BRITISH WILDLIFE
PHOTOGRAPHY AWARDS 13

British Wildlife Photography Awards 13
Published in Great Britain in 2025 by Graffeg Limited.

Text and photographs by British Wildlife Photography Awards copyright © 2025. Designed and produced by Graffeg Limited copyright © 2025.

Graffeg Limited, 24 Stradey Park Business Centre, Mwrwg Road, Llangennech, Llanelli, Carmarthenshire, SA14 8YP, Wales, UK. www.graffeg.com.

British Wildlife Photography Awards is hereby identified as the author of this work in accordance with section 77 of the Copyright, Designs and Patents Act 1988.

A CIP Catalogue record for this book is available from the British Library.

All rights reserved. No part of this publication may be reproduced, stored in a retrieval system or transmitted, in any form or by any means, electronic, mechanical, photocopying, recording or otherwise, without the prior permission of the publishers.

The publisher gratefully acknowledges the financial support of this book by the Books Council of Wales. www.gwales.com.

ISBN 9781802589856

1 2 3 4 5 6 7 8 9

Cover image:
Atlantic Puffin by Matthew Watkinson. Page 50.

BRITISH WILDLIFE

PHOTOGRAPHY AWARDS 13

FOREWORD BY
EVANNA LYNCH

EDITED BY
WILL NICHOLLS

GRAFFEG

CATEGORIES AND AWARDS

Animal Behaviour – Images that convey wildlife behaviour and action.

Animal Portrait – Images that capture the beauty and 'character' of the subject, often showcasing the 'personality' of an animal.

Botanical Britain – Images of trees, plants, flowers, fungi and algae that showcase the diversity of the botanical world.

Black & White – Images of British wildlife or landscapes that use this medium creatively, such as highlighting texture and tone.

Coast & Marine – Images showcasing nature beneath the waves.

Habitat – Images that portray the relationship between an environment and the animals that live there.

Hidden Britain – Images that show the life of invertebrates on a small scale.

Urban Wildlife – Images showing wild animals or plants within an urban environment.

Wild Woods – Images that celebrate the beauty and sheer splendour of British woodlands and their residents.

SPECIAL AWARDS

British Seasons – A sequence of four images that show British wildlife at its best across all four seasons.

Documentary Series – A sequence of up to six images of any British wildlife, habitat or landscape conservation issue.

Young British Wildlife Photographer of the Year – Celebrating the talent of photographers under the age of 18, this award is split into three age groups:
11 and under
12-14 years
15-17 years

For further information about the annual competition and touring exhibition please visit:
www.bwpawards.org

CONTENTS

Foreword by Evanna Lynch	6
The British Wildlife Photography Awards	8
Judges	11

Competition photographs including the following images:

British Wildlife Photographer of the Year 2025 Winner	12-13
Urban Wildlife Winner – Simon Withyman	12-13
Habitat Winner – Drew Buckley	17
Black & White Winner – Mark Kirkland	21
Coast & Marine Winner – Nicholas More	25
Hidden Britain Winner – Daniel Trim	111
Botanical Britain Winner – Jacob J. Watson-Howland	133
Animal Portraits Winner – David Tipling	156
Animal Behaviour Winner – John Waters	160
Wild Woods Winner – James Roddie	190
British Seasons Winner – Lauren McIntyre	222
Documentary Series Winner – Chris O'Reilly	226
11 and Under Winner – Jamie Smart	233
15-17 Years Winner – Ben Lucas	236
12-14 Years Winner – Kiran Simpson	238
Index	240

FOREWORD

Evanna Lynch, Actress and Writer.
Photo by Faye Thomas.

One of my favourite things to do on a spare Saturday afternoon is sit on a bench in the local park, look skywards and watch the squirrels.
When autumn leaves crumble away revealing the stark silhouettes of winter is when you really get to see their antics play out in the treetops, and oh, what a show! They are jesters, peering down at dogs, making strange clicking noises that sound very much like cackling. They are the finest of acrobats, their rippling forms streaking confidently along flimsy branches and just as you fear they'll lose their footing they perform a heart-stopping leap across an empty expanse of sky before sticking a landing that would humble an Olympian gymnast. It is a breathtaking spectacle, and I watch, unable to peel my eyes away, until they disappear from view, their bodies spiralling around a distant network of branches.

Beyond the park walls, the city of London glints and simmers menacingly, threatening to encroach on the beauty and serenity, but it does not, and it cannot because there are too many people pushing back against the rabid appetite of consumerism that demands more and more of the Earth's wild spaces. There are too many of us sitting on park benches studying squirrels or belly down for hours in the long grass clutching a camera and thinking: 'this is precious; this is enough'.

The world of humans out of sync with nature is fast, harsh and exhausting. Too much information is transmitted too quickly, saturating our minds and creating rifts that alienate us from one another, let alone from the animal kingdom. Sitting on the park bench, looking up at the sky where branches sway in apparent conversation with one another, I find myself wishing we could move at the pace of trees. I long for their silences to permeate the endless stream of noise so we can hear their whispered wisdom, so we can simply hear ourselves think.

But the natural world is not a utopia either and as these pages show, it is not meant to be. For every field of fragrant lavender there is a jagged barren snowscape where the frail do not survive the winter. For every shimmering young trout, a beady-eyed heron lurks in the reeds. In the woods the big brown eyes of a litter of cubs peer out shyly from the tree trunks while on the streets a world-weary adult fox glares back challengingly. There is life and death in these pages. Decay and rebirth. Beauty and brutality. Nature is not bloodless… but it always is in balance.

I worry often that we won't maintain the delicate balance of the ecosystem that nature manages so effortlessly. I look for proof everywhere that we will wield our considerable intellect wisely to protect the wildlife. I fight to override my own selfish urges to pluck feathered ducklings out of ponds and clutch them to my chest, to wrap squealing pygmy shrews in the folds of my jumper and bring them back to the hearth, to capture and keep impossibly delicate, wondrous creatures clasped forever within my hands.

Our love of the natural world often lies in conflict with the belief that it must be respected, and I don't know if I trust humankind to employ the wisdom needed to curtail our desire for power, beauty and dominion; I don't know if I trust even myself.

Looking at the stunning transient moments captured within the pages of the *British Wildlife Photography Awards* fills me with a new optimism, however, for the symbiotic relationship we can have with the natural world if we can take our place amidst it, let it revive our jaded souls and remember our true nature. Because there must be a reason for this ceaseless curiosity to explore the wild, there must be a reason we all hear that call. The call that urges us to follow foxes down moodily lit allies at night; to stop dead in the middle of a field and lock eyes with a hare; to kneel before the formidable beauty of swans. If we still have this insatiable curiosity, year after year, that pulls us continuously back to explore and embrace the wild, wouldn't that suggest that rather than being trespassers, we are an intrinsic part of it?

For me, a human in constant flux and conflict, I am most struck by the people we can sense behind the camera, their silence total, their gaze focused, the people who slowed down to the pace of the trees, listened to what nature chose to reveal; who show us that animals, plants and people all have an integral role to play in the vast and mysterious landscape of the wild, and we have so much to share with one another. As usual, the artists held the vision for a more beautiful world, and in these pages they have exposed it gloriously.

Evanna Lynch

Cautious Muntjac ▶
Animal Portraits

James MacKinnon
Reeves's muntjac (*Muntiacus reevesi*)
Kings Lynn, Norfolk, England

Canon R5 with Canon EF 500mm f/4L II lens and 1.4x teleconverter. 700mm; 1/320th second; f/5.6; ISO 2,500.

I was lying on the ground of a footpath between the edge of a crop field and a ditch, waiting for deer to appear in the channel. A muntjac buck popped out, he hadn't picked up my scent or noticed my lens poking out of my camo bag hide. Positioned at the top of a slope, the buck cautiously approached. He soon filled the frame with his inquisitive gaze before retreating back into the safety of the crops. Muntjac are shy deer and an introduced species that is now widespread across England and parts of Wales.

THE BRITISH WILDLIFE PHOTOGRAPHY AWARDS

As we unveil collection 13 of the British Wildlife Photography Awards (BWPA), we are once again reminded of the breathtaking beauty and diversity that lies within Britain's natural world. Each year, the competition reveals a unique window into life in our wild spaces – from the serenity of woodland scenes to the vibrant energy of coastal habitats and beyond.

This year, we received an astounding number of entries, each image serving as a powerful testament to the resilience and brilliance of British wildlife. With so many talented photographers participating, this collection represents not only their technical excellence but also their dedication to understanding and capturing the essence of nature.

Nature photography is not just about mastering the use of a camera or composing the perfect shot. A strong technical skillset is merely the foundation. The photographers showcased within these pages have dedicated countless hours to honing their fieldcraft – learning how to move through the environment with minimal disturbance. This careful approach ensures that the images captured reflect authentic and natural behaviours, offering us, as admirers, a genuine glimpse into nature through their unique perspectives.

Beyond its visual splendour, this collection stands as a call to action. It inspires us to cherish and protect the natural spaces that are so integral to Britain's identity. Through these pages, we invite you to explore, appreciate and connect with the untamed beauty of Britain's wildlife.

Let this book be more than a celebration; let it be a catalyst. Engage with conservation efforts, support local initiatives and immerse yourself in the landscapes and species that make Britain so extraordinary. Together, even the smallest actions can make a lasting difference in safeguarding our shared natural heritage.

Will Nicholls, Director

Koi
Hidden Britain | Runner-up

David Maitland
Cinnabar moth (*Tyria jacobaeae*)
Thetford Forest, Norfolk, England

Sony A7R II with Olympus BX51 Microscope (200x Magnification). 1.3 seconds; ISO 100; stacked image.

Resembling goldfish or koi carp swimming in a pond, these are the wing scales of the cinnabar moth. Photographed under ultraviolet (UV) light, the scales that appear red in visible light fluoresce red under UV, while those that appear black in daylight do not fluoresce at all and remain jet-black.

In the Beginning
Hidden Britain

Julian Terreros-Martin
Common frog (*Rana temporaria*)
Messingham, Lincolnshire, England

Canon R3 with Laowa 24mm f/14 Probe lens. 14mm; 1/400th second; ISO 4,000.

During the COVID lockdowns in 2020, I made a reflection pool in my back garden to photograph garden birds when we were unable to travel for photography. Four years on, the reflection pool is no longer used for photography but has been taken over by nature. I noticed some frogs had spawned in the pool of water and I thought it would be a perfect opportunity to use my probe lens in the shallow water. I used an underwater torch to light them from behind to create backlighting. Capturing the development of the eggs was incredibly interesting, seeing how they start to develop features we see from their tadpole stage.

JUDGES

Alex Mustard MBE
Alex is an underwater photographer with a Ph.D. in marine ecology. He is a six-time category winner in BWPA and highly regarded around the world, receiving an MBE from Queen Elizabeth II for services to underwater photography.

Dani Connor
Dani is a wildlife photographer and an online content creator. She shares her journey photographing wildlife through YouTube videos and her mission is to connect and engage people with the natural world.

Margot Raggett MBE
Margot left a corporate PR career in London in 2010 to concentrate on her love of wildlife photography. She was 'Photographer in Residence' at Entim Camp in the Maasai Mara and also led photographic safaris before founding the Remembering Wildlife series of fundraising photography books in 2015, which have raised over £1.1m for conservation projects in 32 countries.

Margot was awarded an MBE in the June 2023 King's Birthday Honours List for services to international wildlife conservation.

Ross Hoddinott
Ross is one of the UK's best-known landscape and nature photographers and authors. Specialising in intimate close-ups of insects and plant life, Ross is a previous winner of BWPA. Ross lives in north Cornwall with his family where they have rewilded several acres of land to encourage local wildlife to thrive.

Will Nicholls
Will is the director of BWPA. He is also a wildlife cameraman working in natural history television for major broadcasters including Netflix, Disney, and Apple TV+. He has been a stills photographer since 2007.

OVERALL WINNER

Urban Explorer
British Wildlife Photographer of the Year 2025
and Winner of Urban Wildlife

Simon Withyman
Red fox (*Vulpes vulpes*)
Bristol, England

Canon R5 with Canon EF 24-70mm f/2.8L II lens.
39mm; 1/400th second; f/2.8; ISO 640.

For approximately three years, I had been photographing this vixen and was able to track her movements across the city. Surprisingly, she covered large distances, eventually moving over a mile away from her original parental territory. In the city, that means a lot of roads, hazards and other fox territories to contend with. This streetwise fox was a successful mother and had a family of young mouths to feed. She would patrol the streets and the area near her den searching for food for herself and her young family. She would opportunistically hunt rodents and birds, as well as scavenge takeaway leftovers dropped on the floor. I wanted to capture a creative environment portrait as she went about her daily routine. I was instantly drawn to the interesting perspective effect of these railings and wanted to showcase some beauty in this everyday urban scene.

Simon Withyman
Simon is a UK-based creative photographer driven by a passion for wildlife and creating storytelling images. He has been involved in several long-term projects that focus on species that call the UK home. His goal is to reveal the unique personalities of individuals as they navigate their way through life.

Golden Grouse
Habitat | Highly Commended

Ben Hall
Red grouse (*Lagopus lagopus scotica*)
Peak District National Park, England

Canon 1D X Mark II with Canon EF 500mm f/4L lens.
500mm; 1/2,500th second; f/4; ISO 400.

I spent several weeks one summer photographing red grouse at first light, aiming to capture these stunning birds backlit against the heather and grasses of the Peak District moorlands. On this particular morning, the conditions were perfect. As the sun crested the horizon, the moor was bathed in golden light, providing an ideal backdrop for an environmental study.

The Morning Sun
Habitat | Highly Commended

Amanda Cook
Red deer (*Cervus elaphus*)
Bushy Park, England

Nikon D850 with Nikon 70-300mm f/4.5-5.6 lens. 70mm; 1/500th second; f/13; ISO 200.

On a beautiful May morning at dawn, I ventured into Bushy Park, hoping to photograph the deer. After walking around for some time, I finally came upon a group of deer standing guard beneath an oak tree. On the farthest deer, you can just make out a jackdaw perched on its neck. At this time of year, jackdaws often gather fur from the deer for nest building.

Hardy Hare
Habitat

James Roddie
Mountain hare (*Lepus timidus*)
Cairngorms, Scotland

Nikon Z 9 with Nikon 500mm f/4 lens. 500mm; 1/1,250th second; f/4; ISO 400.

A heavy fall of dry snow followed by strong winds often produces exceptional conditions for photography. I headed up into the hills to look for mountain hares and found this individual sitting in a perfect location. As a gusty squall passed through, the wind speeds increased dramatically, sending plumes of spindrift over the hare. I shot a large number of frames in a short amount of time, hoping to capture a plume of spindrift just as it hit the hare's back. I got back to my car extremely cold and with a camera covered in ice, but I was delighted with the images I had captured.

Kingdom of the Hare
Habitat | Winner

Drew Buckley
Mountain hare (*Lepus timidus*)
Highlands, Scotland

Canon 1D X with Canon EF 24-70mm f/2.8L II lens. 47mm; 1/1,600th second; f/10; ISO 1,000.

After a lot of trudging through deep snow high in the Monadhliath Mountains, Scotland, I came across this one individual hare hunkered down in its form. Sheltered from the bitterly cold wind, I spent a while capturing different scenes and focal lengths from a distance before moving on.

Surfing
Black & White

Kirsty Andrews
Grey seal (*Halichoerus grypus*)
Sula Sgeir, Scotland

Nikon D500 with Tokina 10-17mm f/3.5-4.5 Fisheye lens. 17mm; 1/250th second; f/14; ISO 500.

Around the remote outpost of Sula Sgeir, an uninhabited island many miles from the Scottish mainland, grey seals are unaccustomed to human visitors. I watched several seals play effortlessly in the surf zone. I loved the drama of the rolling waves overhead but had to clutch the kelp holdfasts tightly to take this shot.

Shark and Sunbeams
Black & White | Highly Commended

Gillian Marsh
Blue shark (*Prionace glauca*)
Penzance, Cornwall, England

Canon 5D Mark III with Canon EF 8-15mm f/4L Fisheye lens. 15mm; 1/200th second; f/14; ISO 400.

This photograph was taken around 12 miles offshore from Penzance in Cornwall on the second of two amazing days of snorkelling over the August Bank Holiday. The sea was calm, there was no wind and the sun shone. We had created a chum slick to attract the blue sharks, but we had everything that day, including dolphins, a large school of bluefin tuna and a basking shark. We even saw a bait ball in the distance.

Underwater Flight
Black & White | Highly Commended

Henley Spiers
Guillemot (*Uria aalge*)
St Abbs, Scotland

Nikon D850 with Nikon 28-70mm f/3.5-4.5 lens.
45mm; 1/15th second; f/22; ISO 125.

A guillemot swims by at speed underwater as it hunts for food. These seabirds use rapid beats of their wings to 'fly' underwater with impressive agility. As we dived beneath them, our bubbles attracted the seabirds, perhaps mistaken for the small, silvery fish they feed on. I used a slow shutter speed and intentional camera movement to capture the dynamism of their behaviour.

Guillemot Kingdom
Black & White | Winner

Mark Kirkland
Guillemot (*Uria aalge*)
St Abbs, Scotland

Nikon D500 with Tokina 10-17mm f/3.5-4.5
Fisheye lens. 14mm; 1/160th second; f/14; ISO 160.

Photographing guillemots underwater is a seasonal treat for divers. Through early summer, they congregate in huge numbers along the cliffs of the Berwickshire coast to breed. They are often attracted to divers in the water, the leading theory being that they mistake divers' bubbles for their primary food source, shoals of tiny sand eels. The foot of the towering cliffs is only accessible by boat, this time sailing out from St Abbs. For over an hour, I sat in one spot among the kelp in eight metres of water, waiting for their curiosity to pique.

Beach Patrol
Habitat

Terry Whittaker
Pine marten (*Martes martes*)
Black Isle, Scotland

Nikon D600 with Nikon 24-85mm f/3.5-4.5 lens. 24mm; 1/160th second; f/10; ISO 200.

I set two DSLR camera traps along this secluded beach on the Black Isle in Scotland with the intention of photographing otters. To my surprise, over a period of around two weeks, I didn't get an otter, but I did get several images of this pine marten. From what I can gather from the tracks I found, the marten leaves the forest just above the beach to forage along the tideline. I set this camera between two large rocks, which I thought would be a likely path for otters to take as they leave the beach. No bait was used.

Delta

Botanical Britain | Runner-up

David Maitland
Hypoglossum sp.
St Andrews Bay, Scotland

Sony A7R IV with 10x Microscope Objective. 1/13th second; ISO 100; stacked image.

This red seaweed, washed up after a storm, reveals a network of strengthened cells arranged as a pattern of fine branches, much like a river delta. Fine details are highlighted by illuminating with UV light.

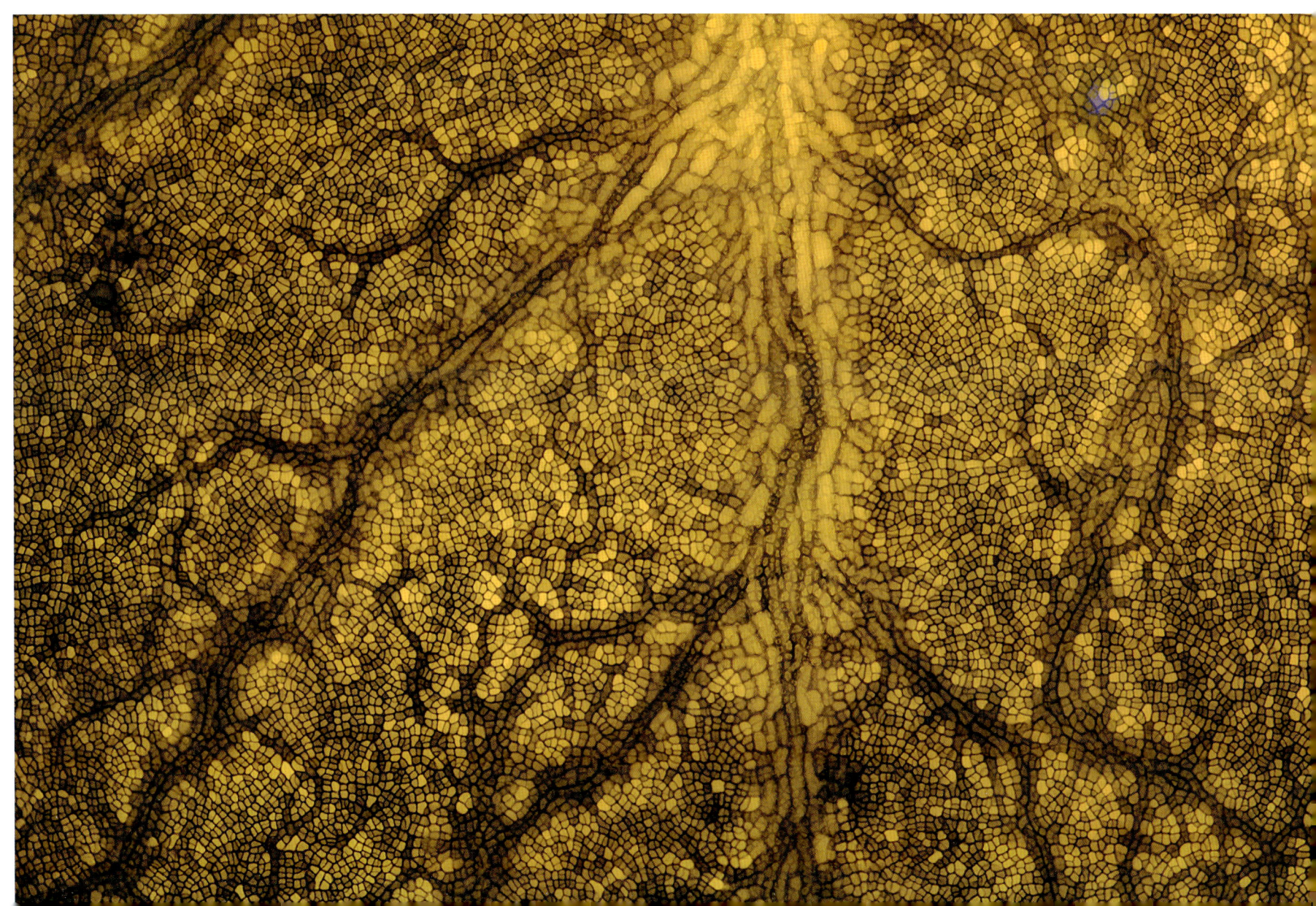

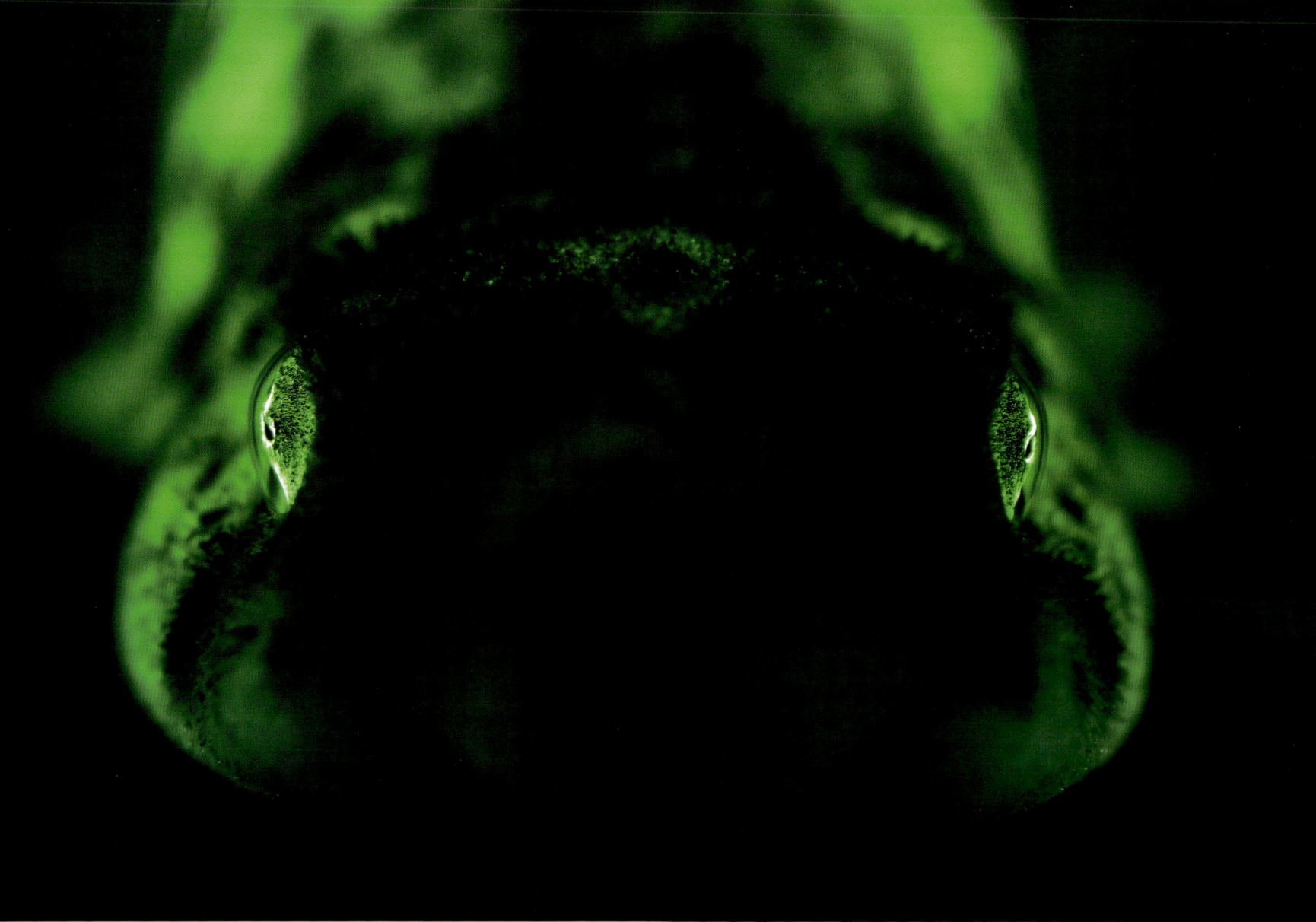

Fluo Shark Eyes
Coast & Marine

James Lynott
Small-spotted catshark (*Scyliorhinus canicula*)
Loch Long, Scotland

Canon G7X III with Nauticam CMC1 wet lens.
26mm; 1/100th second; f/5; ISO 400.

This shot was captured during a night dive in Loch Long in March 2024. During the first dive of the evening, I spotted this juvenile small-spotted catshark on the seabed and took a few quick normal shots of it before leaving it in peace. Thankfully, on my second dive (with fluo gear this time), the shark hadn't moved at all, and I was able to find it again.

Blue Shark
Coast & Marine | Winner

Nicholas More
Blue shark (*Prionace glauca*)
Penzance, Cornwall, England

Nikon D850 with Nikon 8-15mm f/3.5-4.5 lens. 15mm; 1/8th second; f/20; ISO 80.

This slow-shutter speed portrait of a blue shark was captured ten to fifteen miles southwest of Penzance, Cornwall. Blue sharks are summer, seasonal visitors to UK waters. They are bold and curious sharks that are inquisitive and interactive with snorkelers. Blue sharks feed on small fish and squid and are readily attracted to boats using Rubby Dubby, a mixture of dead fish carcasses, oils, and bran. As such, these apex predators are particularly susceptible to long-line fishing and, with no catch limits or quotas, are overexploited for their fins in the production of shark fin soup. These beautiful oceanic animals deserve our protection.

The Rain-Deer

Animal Behaviour | Runner-up

Paul Browning

Red deer (*Cervus elaphus*)
Surrey, England

Sony A1 with Sony FE 400mm f/2.8 GM lens. 400mm; 1/250th second; f/2.8; ISO 500.

At the end of September and up until December, I spend as much time as possible with the red deer, following them through all the stages of the rut in Bushy Park and Richmond Park in south England. After one of my social meet-ups with my Instagram friends, we were just getting ready to leave the park when the heavens opened! So instead of covering my camera, I thought this was the ideal chance to capture the pouring rain using a slower shutter speed than usual, just hoping one of the stags would put on a show with a roar... and this was that moment! I love this photo because of that, but also because my dad has it as his computer screensaver – he loves it so much!

Razorbill Rainstorm
Animal Portraits

Finley Dennison
Razorbill (*Alca torda*)
Isle of May, Scotland

Nikon D500 with Nikon 300mm f/2.8 lens and 1.4x teleconverter. 420mm; 1/125th second; f/6.3; ISO 720.

A torrential rainstorm on the Isle of May during the summer breeding season presented a unique opportunity to photograph the seabirds that inhabited the island in a different way. So I donned my waterproofs and trekked across the island to a spot where I'd have the best chance of seeing razorbills up on the top of the cliff. I only had a short window to get the shot before my camera became too wet to continue, and using a long shutter speed, I was able to capture the raindrops as long streaks set against the dark, moody sea cliffs behind.

Harrier Agility
Animal Behaviour | Highly Commended

Dave Wesson
Marsh harrier (Circus aeruginosus)
RSPB Blacktoft Sands, England

Nikon Z 9 with Nikon Z 800mm f/6.3 lens. 800mm; 1/2,500th second; f/8; ISO 1,600.

After sitting in a hide for several hours watching a male marsh harrier hunting and then performing food passes to the female, who then took the food back to the nest to feed the chicks, I couldn't believe it when I saw the male chasing a baby blue tit and trying to catch it in mid-air, as I'd never seen this before. It was all over in a fraction of a second and, fortunately, I had the required settings dialled in on my camera to capture this rare behaviour.

Flying at the Right Angle
Black & White | Highly Commended

Eden Davies
Common swift (*Apus apus*)
Barnstaple, England

Nikon Z 9 with Nikon 500mm f/5.6 PF lens. 500mm; 1/4,000th second; f/5.6; ISO 640.

This photograph aimed to highlight the aerodynamic wonder of the swift from an unusual perspective. A small colony of swifts returns each spring to my village to breed. After observing their behaviour, I began to predict their flight paths low over the houses. Even though I could position myself in a favourable spot with swifts regularly flying low over me, their supreme agility and speed meant it took many, many attempts to capture the image I was looking for. The high contrast of the image made it perfect for conversion into a high-key black-and-white image.

A Short Pose
Animal Portraits

Lauren McIntyre
Short-eared owl (*Asio flammeus*)
Norfolk, England

Nikon D850 with Sigma 150-600mm f/5-6.3 Contemporary lens. 600mm; 1/2,000th second; f/6.3; ISO 2,000.

I couldn't resist trying a nearby spot while on holiday in Norfolk. The sun had come out after a few days of rain, and I had a feeling that the short-eared owls would be out too, making the most of the nice weather. It's a privilege to be able to watch these owls hunt in their natural, unspoilt habitat. The setting sun provided beautiful light and colours. Then, when I thought it couldn't get any better, this owl gave me its closest fly-by of the day, turning its head to look right at me as it went by. Simply magical.

Will it Ever Stop Raining
Animal Portraits

Phill Gwilliam
Little owl (*Athene noctua*)
North Norfolk, England

Nikon D500 with Nikon 500mm f/5.6 PF lens.
500mm; 1/250th second; f/6.3; ISO 800.

It was late May and a day of relentless heavy rain showers. As I pulled up in my car at a location where I'd previously seen little owls, it was pouring down. Almost immediately, I spotted the owl sitting in a corner of a broken window. I quickly began taking images from the seat of the car. As I watched through the camera lens, I got the impression that the bird was thinking as I was, 'Will it ever stop raining?'

Peek-a-boo, We See You
Animal Portraits

Robert Collins
Red fox (*Vulpes vulpes*)
Templecombe, Somerset, England

Nikon D500 with Nikon 200-500mm f/5.6 lens. 500mm; 1/250th second; f/5.6; ISO 1,600.

It's the pandemic, under the first lockdown. My closest friend and I, both key workers fortunate enough to live in the countryside, were out in nature, socially distanced but able to do the thing that brings us joy. As we walked across the fields, we caught a glimpse of a single little cub peering out at us from across a stream. We tucked ourselves quietly beneath a hedgerow. More cubs began to venture above ground. This image shows three adorable siblings looking out from their earth in curiosity as they clamber out to play under the evening sky.

Surrounded by Memories
Urban Wildlife

Alex Witt
Roe deer (*Cervus elaphus*)
Surrey, England

Canon 1D X Mark II with Canon EF 500mm f/4L II lens. 500mm; 1/400th second; f/4; ISO 2,000.

This was the dominant buck in the cemetery for several years, with a very distinctive large and wide set of antlers. This particular year, one of the points of his impressive antlers had broken off, possibly in a fight to defend his prized territory. The towering old gravestones and memorials serve to highlight the diminutive size of the roe deer as a species whilst also framing a scene of life amongst death and nature adapting and flourishing in an urban setting.

Rainbow Trout Circle
Animal Portraits

Jenny Stock
Rainbow trout (*Oncorhynchus mykiss*)
River Test, Stockbridge, England

Nikon D4 with Nikon 15mm f/2.8 lens. 15mm; 1/250th second; f/10; ISO 800.

These stunning rainbow trout will patrol the River Test looking for insects on the surface to feast upon. When insects are abundant, they jump into action, competing for their next delicious meal. I captured this image with a unique camera rig designed to take photos remotely. This means you can monitor and capture images from the side of a river without disturbing these shy fish.

Urban Rainbow
Urban Wildlife | Highly Commended

Paul Colley
Rainbow trout (*Oncorhynchus mykiss*)
Whitchurch Silk Mill, Hampshire, England

Nikon D4 with Nikon 16-35mm f/4 lens. 16mm; 1/320th second; f/13; ISO 1,250.

A rainbow trout swimming in the River Test at Whitchurch Silk Mill in Hampshire. This non-native freshwater fish is long established in this precious chalk stream habitat and prized by many fishermen. However, its habitat is under threat from sewage dumping and run-off from housing, transport and agricultural sources. Silk Mill staff and local volunteers take great pride in caring for this particular stretch of water. An experimental in-camera double exposure merged above- and underwater scenes to overcome traditional depth-of-field and exposure limitations while creating this insight into what swims in the Silk Mill waters.

A Time to Reflect
Habitat

Thomas Roberts
Water vole (*Arvicola amphibius*)
Fowlmere, England

Canon 5D Mark IV with Canon EF 500mm f/4L lens. 500mm; 1/250th second; f/5.6; ISO 12,800.

I had not photographed a water vole before, so I decided to spend the day focusing on this species. The hours passed, and I was not having much luck. The evening came, and I began my return to the car, walking along the chalk stream edge, when I suddenly noticed one in the vegetation just inches from my foot. I stood still and waited. The vole then swam across the stream, so I got down low and began to take photos. The water created a lovely reflection; I couldn't have gotten luckier. It was an amazing moment.

Pembrokeshire Bluebells
Wild Woods | Highly Commended

Drew Buckley
Bluebells and Beech trees (*Hyacinthoides non-scripta* and *Fagus sp.*)
Pembrokeshire, Wales

Canon 5D Mark IV with Canon EF 24-70mm f/2.8L II lens. 63mm; 0.8 seconds; f/16; ISO 100.

The evening sun shines through a beech woodland in springtime. Getting to the woods early enough to scout potential compositions then waiting for the sun to get low enough for it to cast light through the trunks, I always like capturing the sun peeking out from behind elements in the frame and using a small aperture to capture natural sun stars.

Winter Hold
Wild Woods

Graham Niven
Silver birch (*Betula pendula*)
Cairngorms, Scotland

Nikon D850 with Nikon 20mm f/1.8 lens. 20mm; 1/250th second; f/6.3; ISO 64.

In early winter, after a few days of deep cold frosts, everything was covered in hoar frost. This forms when the water vapour in the air comes into contact with solid surfaces that are already below freezing point. Ice crystals form immediately and continue to grow as more water vapour freezes.

An inversion meant that I had to climb higher through the forest to find this scene. The mist was wonderfully atmospheric, but breaking through to see this world of crystallised statues against the deep blue sky was mesmerising. Amongst many images of the birch forest I took that day, this vision, looking directly up, is always one that draws my eye – finding a group of trees that compose well together as their frozen, tendril-like branches reach out towards a window of blue, an image I often capture from lying on my back.

Fungi Forager
Hidden Britain

Tim Crabb
Springtail (*Lepidocyrtus violaceus*)
Bridford Wood, Dartmoor National Park, Devon, England

Canon R5 with Canon MP-65mm f/2.8 1-5x Macro lens. 65mm; 1/100th second; f/7.1; ISO 1,600.

In a world often overlooked, a type of springtail called *Lepidocyrtus violaceus*, a delicate and iridescent creature, rests on a group of lemon discos. Its slender form contrasts beautifully against the vibrant hues of the fungi, mixing a vibrant array of colours and textures. This tiny arthropod adds a magical touch to the scene, showing us how nature surprises us in unexpected places.

Tawny Owlet Branchling
Animal Portraits

Lauren McIntyre
Tawny owl (*Strix aluco*)
Micheldever Woods, England

Nikon D850 with Sigma 150-600mm f/5-6.3 Contemporary lens. 600mm; 1/80th second; f/6.3; ISO 800.

I'd found this tawny owlet the day before, sitting low in the tree, and as I left it, I'd jokingly said I'd be very grateful if it felt like hopping over to the bluebells before I came back tomorrow. Well, you can imagine my absolute shock and elation when I returned the next morning to find it sitting snoozing on a fallen branch with the bluebells behind it! I sat and waited for the rising sun to shine through and naturally light the owlet, enjoying every single minute of this rare and wonderful encounter. A true pinch-me moment.

The Portal to Heaven
Wild Woods

Christopher Harrison
Bluebells and Beech trees
(*Hyacinthoides non-scripta* and *Fagus sp.*)
Chilterns AONB, England

Sony A7R IV with Sigma 24-70mm f/2.8 Art lens.
30mm; 1/4th second; f/22; ISO 100.

After many early mornings spent scouting for the perfect composition with the right characteristics, I found this hidden gem close to home. The season's poor weather brought numerous failed attempts at capturing the right conditions, turning this into a tale of perseverance and resilience. This ancient beech copse, tucked away, became my chosen location, shared only with the deer, owls and squirrels that inhabit it during the early sunrises. On this particular morning, late in the bluebell season, when spiders had begun to lace webs in the flowers, the conditions finally aligned. Fog enveloped the forest, and the sun broke through the trees, casting beautiful light through the trees and across the woodland floor. The sunbeams illuminated the bluebells, creating a springtime scene that was ethereal and almost otherworldly. This wide-angle shot captures the moment when the light transformed the forest, reminding us that the most extraordinary scenes can often be found right in our own backyard.

Paired Up
Animal Portraits

Drew Buckley
Razorbill (*Alca torda*)
Skomer Island, Pembrokeshire, Wales

Canon R5 with Canon RF 100-500mm f/4.5-7.1L lens. 500mm; 1/1,250th second; f/7.1; ISO 1,250.

On Skomer Island, there's plenty of other wildlife to point a lens at. One area is superb for auks, and I captured these razorbills one morning at sunrise. Lining the birds up between myself and the reflected sunrise and using a shallow aperture helped create out-of-focus bokeh balls of light in the sea, adding to the image.

Sibling Affection
Black & White

Mark Nicolaides
Roe deer (*Capreolus capreolus*)
Dorset, England

Nikon D500 with Nikon 500mm f/5.6 PF lens. 500mm; 1/1,250th second; f/5.6; ISO 3,200.

The loss of the twins' mother seemed to accentuate the pair bond between these roe deer and I became particularly keen to capture it. During the winter, the pair became especially nervous and were often difficult to locate, and when they were spotted, more often than not, they'd be found in a scrubby pasture, which made it very challenging to make a good image of them together. Eventually, in April, I was lucky enough to find them in an open area and it was finally possible to take this photograph of them together as they demonstrated the affectionate relationship that existed between the pair.

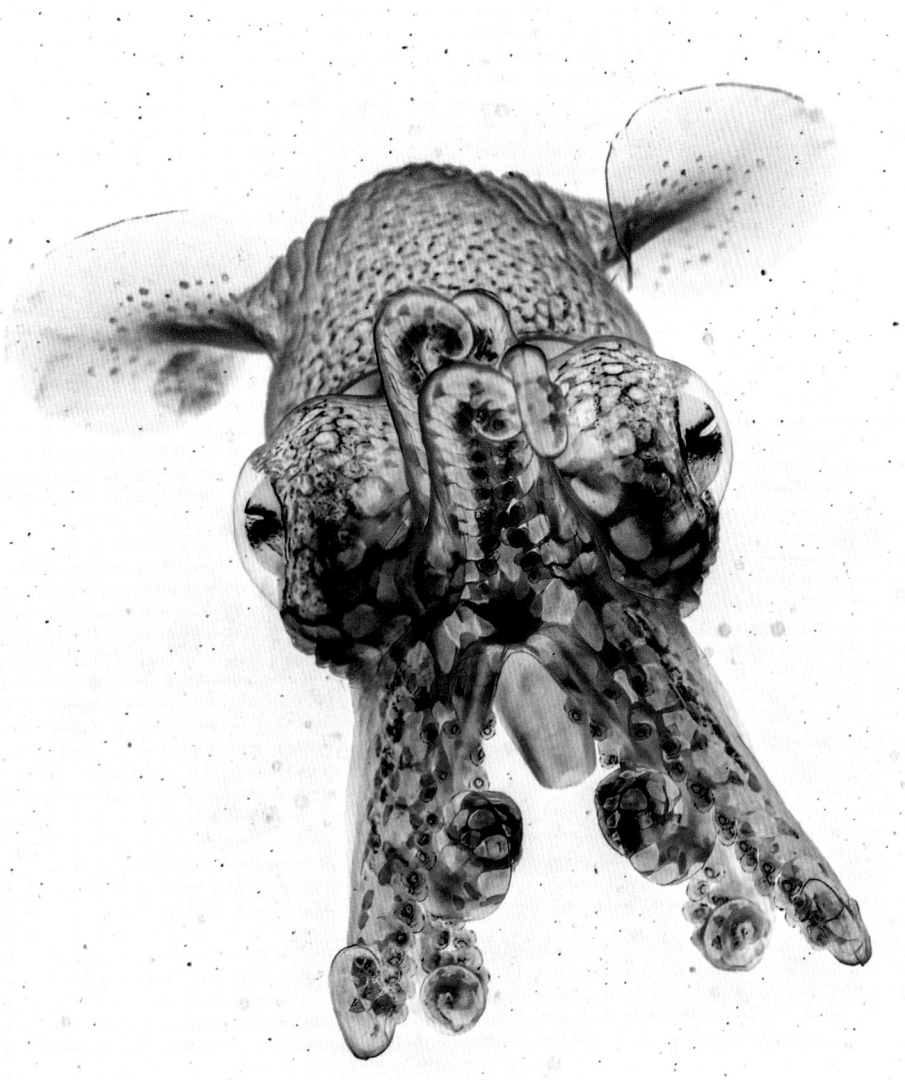

Dumbo
Black & White

Paul Pettitt
Bobtail squid (*Sepiolida*)
Portland Harbour, England

Nikon D500 with Nikon 60mm f/2.8 lens. 60mm; 1/200th second; f/11; ISO 320.

This little bobtail squid was photographed on a night dive at a secluded little site near Weymouth. These are usually best spotted when daylight has completely gone, as they seem to be attracted to the divers' torches. Usually sitting on the sandy bed, they will rise a metre or so and follow the light beam; that is the best time to try to photograph them. This particular shot is unusual as it is face-on, where the norm is to usually get them from the side. I particularly like the resemblance to a famous cartoon character. I decided to leave all the backscatter in the picture, as I think it enhances it.

Laser Focus, Silver Shimmer ▶
Black & White

Nur Tucker
Guillemot (*Uria aalge*)
St Abbs, Scotland

Nikon D500 with Sigma 17-70mm f/2.8-4 lens. 34mm; 1/250th second; f/9; ISO 320.

I took this shot during my first ever cold-water dive in a dry suit. We arrived in St Abbs on a boat, and the sound of the thousands of guillemots filled me with excitement. I took my giant step, looked down with my camera and saw this guillemot diving with serious, laser-focused eyes, looking for prey. The bird's reflections on the surface looked very appealing. Without hesitation, I pressed the shutter. This is the first shot I took on that dive. No bait needed to be used, as guillemots are excellent divers. Their main diet consists of a variety of fish, crustaceans and squid, all of which are abundant in the waters there.

Mountain Meeting
Habitat

Chas Moonie
Mountain hare (*Lepus timidus*)
Cairngorms, Scotland

Canon 5D Mark IV with Canon EF 100-400mm f/4.5-5.6L II lens and 1.4x teleconverter. 560mm; 1/1,250th second; f/9; ISO 640.

The iconic mountain hare is thankfully now a protected species in Scotland, and numbers are increasing. Winter snow, however, is decreasing, and moments like this are always pleasing to watch despite the almost Arctic conditions. This pair of mountain hares approached each other cautiously on the horizon before coming to a standoff for several minutes, allowing me to capture a few shots. Spring was in the air, and these two had other things on their minds as another breeding season approached.

Mountain Silhouettes
Habitat | Highly Commended

Neil McIntyre
Red deer (*Cervus elaphus*)
Knoydart, Western Highlands, Scotland

Nikon D850 with Nikon 24-70mm f/2.8 lens.
32mm; 1/3,200th second; f/8; ISO 640.

This stunning location is one I visit regularly, and when conditions allow it's great to try a shorter lens to include more of the spectacular surroundings. On this occasion, the light was perfect, giving me patches of light on the distant hills and a dramatic sky, ideal for silhouetting the local stags. For this image, I managed to get myself low and below the stags that I had seen making their way down the hill. I waited until they presented themselves on the ridge against the sky, and then I fired off a few frames before they merged into the darker area at the bottom of the picture.

A Dramatic Display
Animal Behaviour

Matthew Glover
Common eider (*Somateria mollissima*)
Seahouses, Northumberland, England

Canon R5 with Canon RF 100-500mm f/4.5-7.1L lens. 500mm; 1/2,000th second; f/7.1; ISO 640.

A male eider throws back its head and lets out its characteristic cooing call as it seeks to attract a mate. This large sea duck provides an entertaining and energetic display in the confines of the sheltered harbour. This image was taken in Seahouses in Northumberland, a busy harbour town and the gateway to the Farne Islands. Eiders are regularly found amongst the boats transporting tourists out to the islands. They are known locally as Cuddy ducks after their association with St Cuthbert, who lived on nearby Lindisfarne.

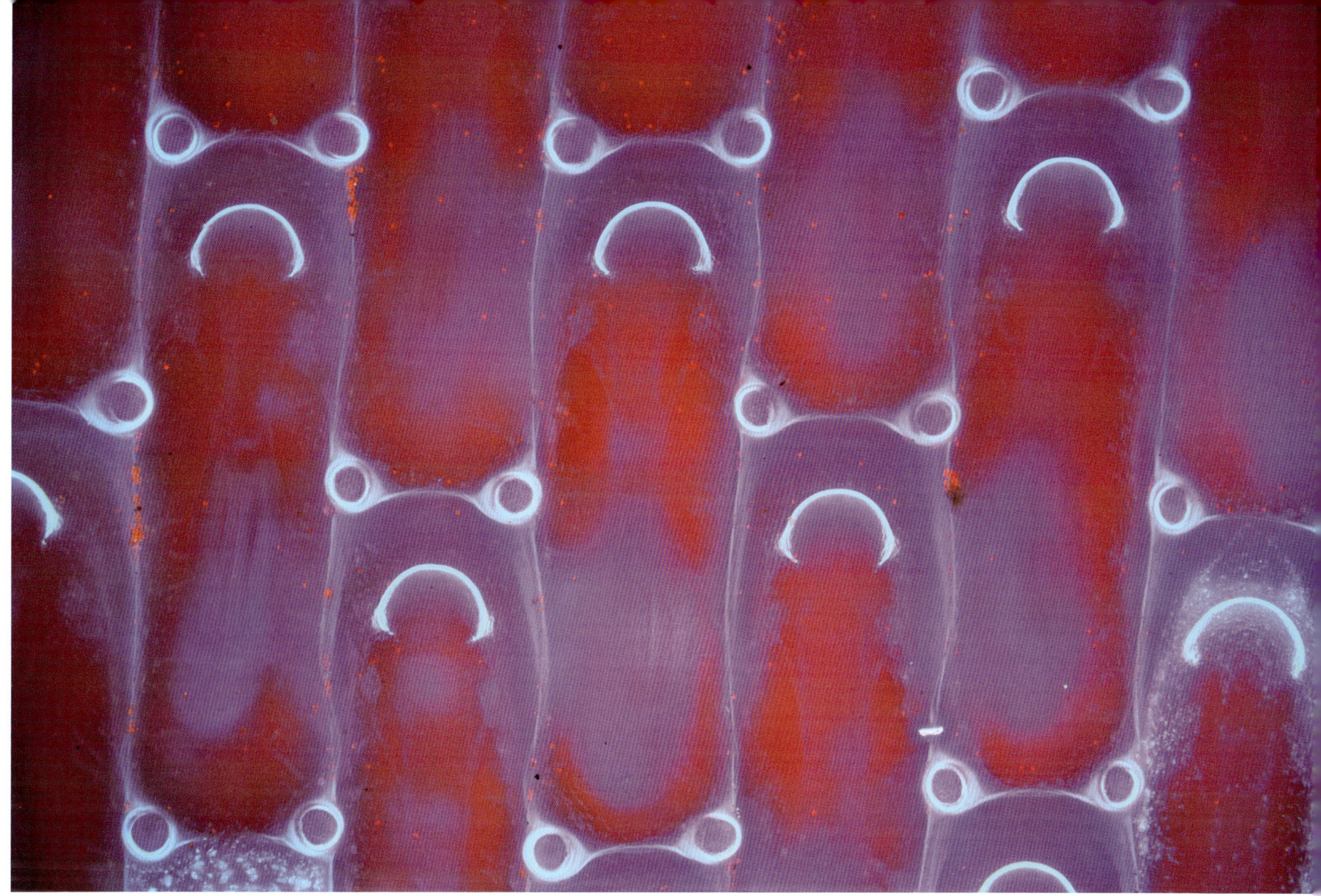

Grumpy
Hidden Britain | Highly Commended

David Maitland
Coffin box bryozoan (*Membranipora membranacea*)
St Andrews Bay, Scotland

Sony A7R IV with Olympus BX51 Microscope (10x Objective). 0.5 seconds; ISO 400; stacked image.

Coffin box bryozoans are colonial animals which typically encrust the flat surface of kelp seaweed. The structure, which looks like a grumpy mouth, is the flap through which the animal extends its feeding tentacles. Fine details are highlighted by illuminating with UV light. The red colour comes from auto-fluorescing chlorophyll present in the kelp and visible through the transparent bodies of the bryozoans.

Atlantic Puffin
Animal Portraits

Matthew Watkinson
Atlantic puffin (*Fratercula arctica*)
Skomer Island, Pembrokeshire, Wales

Canon 90D with Canon EF 100-400mm f/4.5-5.6L II lens. 371mm; 1/125th second; f/6.3; ISO 500.

Sunset on Skomer Island in Pembrokeshire can offer magical opportunities, but I didn't realise what it was doing to the cliffs behind me until I turned around and saw them glowing with this deep orange colour. This incredible phenomenon didn't last more than a few minutes, but luckily there was a puffin posing among the chamomile in just the right place at just the right time, and by lying on the ground I was able to capture this image of the scene.

Puffins in the Pink
Animal Portraits

Robin Lowry
Atlantic puffin (*Fratercula arctica*)
Fair Isle, Scotland

Canon 1D X Mark II with Canon EF 300mm f/2.8L II lens. 300mm; 1/200th second; f/2.8; ISO 1,600.

With barely any time to react to the scene unfolding before me, and hand-holding my camera, I captured a fleeting moment of calm just after sunset. A glorious pink hue adorned the sky, reflecting off the sea in the background of this shot. There were only a few puffins on the clifftop, so I took my time, careful not to rush and disturb them. I moved around to create separation between the two puffins, capturing a scene that looks as if one is calling for the other's attention.

Odd One Out!
Urban Wildlife

Rachel Piper
Common starling (*Sturnus vulgaris*)
Hemel Hempstead, England

Canon 5D Mark IV with Sigma 180mm f/2.8 Macro lens. 180mm; 1/800th second; f/11; ISO 320.

I spent several days in May lying quietly on my garden pod close to my bird feeder. The young starlings and their parents were too busy to notice me as they fought for the prime position on top. This photograph was taken in the morning when the birds were silhouetted against the sky; I think their metal friend caused some confusion!

DIY Mouse
Urban Wildlife | Highly Commended

Robin Lowry
Wood mouse (*Apodemus sylvaticus*)
Stanford-le-Hope, Essex, England

Canon R5 with Sigma 14mm f/1.8 Art lens.
14mm; 1/500th second; f/2.2; ISO 1,000.

I aimed to create an urban environmental image that portrayed this tiny creature in a giant's world, with the mouse as the central subject. I wanted to use a wide-angle lens to capture the depth and scale of the scene, so I opted for my Sigma 14mm f/1.8 Art lens. I used a single Rotolight on a stand to illuminate the scene and used black paper and some tape to control the light spill, creating a more focused spotlight effect. Fortunately, the mouse cooperated perfectly for this shot!

Catch of the Day
Hidden Britain

Tim Hunt
Crab spider (*Misumena Vatia*)
Bournemouth, Dorset, England

Nikon Z 8 with Nikon 105mm f/2.8 Macro lens. 105mm; 1/200th second; f/11; ISO 200.

After discovering this crab spider on the industrial estate where I work, I couldn't wait to capture it on my camera. I had been revisiting the same spot every day over several weeks and, sure enough, it was always there. Upon first discovering it, the spider was white, but over time it gradually turned yellow to match the dandelions it would often be seen on. Each day, it would catch various insects, and on this occasion it had caught a flesh fly.

Close-up Cannibal
Hidden Britain

Will Atkins
Jumping spider (*Aelurillus v-insignitus*)
London, England

Nikon Z 7 with Laowa 90mm f/2.8 2x Macro lens. 90mm; 1/200th second; f/2.8; ISO 1,000.

Everyone likes jumping spiders, with their big forward-facing eyes and their cute teddy-bear bodies, except that they don't hesitate to eat each other, which is not so appealing. At first, I thought this male V-fronted jumping spider, replete with a black-and-white chevron buzzcut, was mating with the smaller female, but instead he had food on his mind. He continued his gruesome meal as I lay down in the tiny patch of urban heathland that is their home while I fired off a series of handheld images that could be stacked to form the final image, showing the events in greater depth.

Redshank
Habitat

Chris Hawes
Redshank (*Tringa totanus*)
Fife Coast, Scotland

Canon 1D X Mark II with Canon EF 300mm f/2.8L II lens and 2x teleconverter. 600mm; 1/640th second; f/5.6; ISO 250.

During a session photographing the waders at my local beach one winter, I took up a position to photograph the birds against the setting sun. I enjoy taking backlit images like this, and I hoped to capture some photographs as the rising tide pushed the birds closer to my position. This redshank obliged by feeding close by, and I was able to take some images in the low late afternoon light.

Misty Sunrise
Animal Portraits

Jeremy Robbins
Great crested grebe (*Podiceps cristatus*)
Eastleigh, Hampshire, England

Canon R6 with Canon RF 600mm f/11 lens. 600mm; 1/1,250th second; f/11; ISO 1,000.

I always check the weather apps for a morning with no wind, no clouds and a promise of mist. This day, all my ducks were in a row (pardon the pun), so I went to the lake before sunrise, waiting for the first light to shine through the trees, casting an orange glow through the mist. Normally, the pair of great crested grebes are in the middle of the lake, but to my surprise one surfaced in front of me and gradually moved through the light for a brief moment before diving again, surfacing a long way away.

Winter's Tale
Animal Portraits

Drew Buckley
Red kite (*Milvus milvus*)
Rhayader, Wales

Canon 5D Mark IV with Canon EF 500mm f/4L lens. 500mm; 1/2,500th second; f/4; ISO 1,000.

One winter, we were lucky to have a cold and snowy spell, so I raced up to one of the well-known red kite feeding centres in Mid Wales to capture these magnificent birds. Come feeding time, more snow showers came through, adding great atmosphere to the shots. Focusing on the birds through the snowfall was a bit hit-and-miss, but I managed to come away with some keepers.

Encrusted
Botanical Britain | Highly Commended

Philip Selby
Snake's-head fritillary (*Fritillaria meleagris*)
Clattinger Farm Nature Reserve, Wiltshire, England

Canon 5D Mark IV with Canon EF 100-400mm f/4.5-5.6L II lens. 321mm; 1/160th second; f/5.6; ISO 400.

After an unseasonably cold and still spring night, I arrived in this Thames Valley meadow in north Wiltshire and was greeted with the most beautiful carpet of frost. Throughout this wonderful hay meadow, a precious remnant of a bygone age, the delicate snake's-head fritillaries were cast rigid, encrusted with jewel-like ice crystals. Knowing that this magical moment would be fleeting once the sun had cast its warming rays, I quickly got into position at ground level and captured this image in the soft, pre-dawn light.

Tethered
Botanical Britain | Highly Commended

David Southern
Kelp (Laminariales)
Northumberland, England

Canon 5D Mark IV with Canon EF 100mm f/2.8L Macro lens. 100mm; 1/13th second; f/16; ISO 100.

My aim was to capture the kelp fronds anchored to the rocks with the water flowing over them. After clambering over slippery boulders to get to the edge of the sea while the tide was at its lowest point, I had to work fast. Kelp is one of the most photogenic of our seaweeds. It has striking metallic colours, rhythmic shapes and is naturally arranged to artistic effect by waves, currents and wind. Being both ubiquitous and perennial, it is accessible throughout the year on almost every rocky shoreline.

Homeward Bound
Animal Portraits

Finley Dennison
Northern gannet (*Morus bassanus*)
Noss, Shetland Islands, Scotland

Nikon D500 with Nikon 24-70mm f/2.8 lens. 56mm; 1/800th second; f/8; ISO 280.

During the breeding season, gannets undertake very long foraging trips in order to provide for their chicks, with some birds travelling hundreds of kilometres from the colony. This shot was captured early one morning, just after sunrise, as a group of gannets was returning to Noss gannetry in the Shetland Islands from their foraging trips out in the North Sea. Using a wide-angle 24-70mm lens, I was able to include the whole group of gannets as well as the dramatic sky.

Sunrise Deer
Animal Portraits

Vai Meng Chan
Fallow deer (*Dama dama*)
Essex, England

Sony A7 IV with Sony FE 400mm f/2.8 GM lens. 400mm; 1/1,250th second; f/2.8; ISO 100.

This was a fleeting moment that went as quickly as it came. In the morning 'magic hour', the young male deer walked right through the golden bokeh, breaking the tranquillity.

Dancing Light
Animal Portraits

Jeremy Robbins
Great crested grebe (*Podiceps cristatus*)
Eastleigh, Hampshire, England

Canon R6 with Canon RF 600mm f/11 lens.
600mm; 1/1,000th second; f/11; ISO 2,000.

As the early morning sun came through the trees, lighting up the mist on the water, a great crested grebe surfaced and moved into the light. A breeze rippled the surface, catching the sun, which danced across the scene. Nobody can enter the water here, and access at water level is limited to a few areas that are mainly fishing swims. I made my own rig to hold the camera and telephoto lens one-handed at arm's length, so while hanging over the swim, I could get the camera close to the water, operating a remote in my other hand.

Dominant Fox
Animal Portraits

Simon Withyman
Red fox (*Vulpes vulpes*)
Bristol, England

Canon R5 with Canon EF 300mm f/2.8L II lens. 300mm; 1/640th second; f/2.8; ISO 160.

After discovering a family of foxes living in an allotment near my home, I frequently visited to learn more about their lives, routines and the characters within the group. This particular fox was the dominant male. During the mating season, he would often be seen patrolling the area and chasing off other foxes from neighbouring territories. During this encounter, he paused to check out a nearby dog walker just outside the allotment boundaries. I was able to frame him using a shallow depth of field, surrounded by an array of colours, from painted sheds to a piece of plastic soil bag flapping in the wind in the foreground.

Witching Hour
Urban Wildlife

Rich Bunce
Red fox (*Vulpes vulpes*)
Chessington, England

Canon 5D Mark IV with Canon EF 24-70mm f/2.8L II lens. 24mm; 15 seconds; f/11; ISO 1,600.

After moving from London to Yorkshire, I realised just how much I'd taken regular fox encounters for granted. Now, whenever visiting my parents, I'll set up a motion sensor camera trap in their garden, hoping to capture their nocturnal visitors. This photo was taken on a Christmas visit, the last night before heading home. Using the camera trap with a mixture of flash and garden lighting, the long exposure allowed the festive lights to appear superimposed over the fox. Camera trapping reminds me of the film photography days – that anticipation of not knowing exactly what you'll get. It's magic.

A Close Encounter
Animal Portraits

Stuart Martinez
Roe deer (*Capreolus capreolus*)
Bispham Green, West Lancashire, England

Nikon Z 9 with Nikon Z 400mm f/2.8 lens. 400mm; 1/1,250th second; f/2.8; ISO 280.

Following a day of heavy rain that gave way to a pleasant evening, I found that roe deer like to come out from the local woods and enjoy the evening sun while grazing in the meadows. On such an occasion, I took a brief walk from home with just the camera and a flask of coffee to enjoy the evening in the hope of encountering a deer or two. Positioning myself under a willow tree with nothing more than the streamside vegetation for cover, I sat quietly and waited. Not long after arriving, I spotted this handsome roe buck coming across the field towards me from the wood on the other side of the field.

It became apparent he knew something was watching him, but instead of running off, he came for a closer look. With my position being downwind of him, he couldn't get my scent and figure out what I was, presenting me with the opportunity to take a number of images using the overhanging willow and foreground vegetation to frame him before he went on his way and began grazing the meadow. A lovely close encounter that I won't forget.

Amongst the Frost and Ferns
Animal Behaviour

Amy Humphries
Fallow deer (*Dama dama*)
Bushy Park, England

Nikon D850 with Sigma 150-600mm f/5-6.3 lens. 460mm; 1/800th second; f/6.3; ISO 6,400.

I spent a frosty morning at the end of October following the herd of fallow deer, moving away from their much noisier red cousins. I noticed that the spider webs and spots of dew had frozen on the beautiful autumnal flora and fauna, and I waited for a solitary black buck to finally raise his head. It was a really special moment; there wasn't another person in sight, and it was worth that 5am alarm.

Crested Tit
Wild Woods | Highly Commended

Danny Green
Crested tit (*Lophophanes cristatus*)
Cairngorms, Scotland

Canon 1D X Mark III with Canon EF 500mm f/4L II lens and 1.4x teleconverter. 700mm; 1/320th second; f/5.6; ISO 800.

One of my favourite birds to be found in the UK is the crested tit. This beautiful bird can only be found in a few areas in the Highlands of Scotland, and it doesn't really expand its range, as it is very sedentary. I spent this winter working with this stunning bird in the Cairngorms region of Scotland.

Garden Help
Animal Portraits

Sarah Darnell
Blue tit (*Cyanistes caeruleus*)
Norfolk, England

Canon R3 with Canon EF 600mm f/4L II lens and 1.4x teleconverter. 840mm; 1/1,250th second; f/5.6; ISO 3,200.

This little blue tit didn't get the memo that it was too cold for gardening that morning. Ever hopeful I would venture outside to the garden with something tasty and warming to eat, it sat on my grandad's old spade handle, left in the flower bed, in eager anticipation of a hearty breakfast. It was hard to resist this sweet appeal, and the feeder was dutifully filled with some suet nibbles for feasting.

Woodland Oasis
Wild Woods | Highly Commended

Robin Dodd
Bridford Wood, Dartmoor National Park, England

Canon R5 with Canon RF 15-35mm f/2.8L lens. 15mm; 0.3 seconds; f/13; ISO 200.

These woods keep drawing me back time and time again. Initially, I had arrived to shoot the bluebells but quickly became distracted by this scene.

Woodland Stop Sign
Botanical Britain

Ben Griffin
Common deceiver (*Laccaria laccata*)
An ancient woodland in Norfolk, England

Canon R7 with Canon EF 100mm f/2.8L Macro lens. 100mm; 1/5th second; f/2.8; ISO 100.

Every autumn, I spend countless hours wandering through ancient woodlands, searching for my favourite subjects to photograph. On this occasion, I discovered a delicate common deceiver mushroom nestled in a bed of damp moss. Fascinated by its intricate beauty, I positioned my camera beneath the mushroom, shooting upward to capture the fine details of its gills. The sunlit foliage in the background added a soft, natural glow, allowing me to create this minimalist photograph using focus stacking to highlight the delicate structure of this woodland treasure.

Morning Breath
Animal Behaviour

Liam Willis
Red deer (*Cervus elaphus*)
Richmond Park, England

Canon 77D with Canon EF 100-400mm f/4.5-5.6L lens. 275mm; 1/400th second; f/10; ISO 200.

Early in October, and during the first frost, mist engulfed most of the Richmond Park ponds. The sounds of the bellowing stags during the rut echoed around the park, so I carefully made my way towards the mating call. Minutes after sunrise, this stag was initially hiding, bellowing from the shrubs. He rose, strutted out 50 metres and let out the biggest and loudest bellow I've ever heard, accompanied by his visible morning breath. Steam emanated from his whole body into the crisp morning air. This is a shot that I'd worked for years to achieve.

Badger Highway
Black & White

Lee Mansfield
Badger (*Meles mele*)
West Sussex, England

Nikon Z 6 II with Nikon Z 70-200mm f/2.8 lens.
88mm; 1/100th second; f/2.8; ISO 1,000.

My local badgers have a habit of using many fallen trees to cross the stream that intersects the woodland they call home. Positioning myself on the stream bed, sitting in complete darkness, I patiently waited for the badger to follow its well-trodden nightly route, using only a single LED light and a silent shutter. The badger crossed the stream and went on its way to forage for another night.

Staggering Beauty
Hidden Britain

George Turner
Stag beetle (*Lucanus cervus*)
Lyndhurst, New Forest, England

Canon 90D with Canon EF 100mm f/2.8L Macro lens. 100mm; 1/80th second; f/13; ISO 800.

Male stag beetles spend much of the day sunning themselves on trees, branches and logs. Exploring a woodland in the New Forest, I encountered this one on a low-lying, moss-covered branch, absorbing the sun's rays and gaining energy for the flights that would commence later that evening. Positioning my camera below this gentle giant helped to portray just how large and impressive these beetles really are.

Baby Snail
Hidden Britain

David Maitland
Dwarf pond snail (*Galbra truncatula*)
St Andrews, Scotland

Sony A7R IV with 10x Microscope Objective.
1/60th second; ISO 400.

Embryonic pond snails graze upon the inside wall of their egg. The snail grows and the shell thins until, finally, the snail breaks free.

Aerial Attack
Animal Behaviour

Tom Broxup
Peregrine falcon and Avocets
(*Falco peregrinus* and *Recurvirostra avosetta*)
Humber Estuary, England

Canon R5 with Canon EF 600mm f/4L II lens and 1.4x teleconverter. 840mm; 1/1,600th second; f/8; ISO 640.

I had spent a morning at Alkborough Flats in Humberside in search of bearded tits with little success. I decided to take a walk along the Humber Estuary to look for some waders and do a little bit of birdwatching. I found around 200 avocets feeding on the exposed mudflats, as the tide was out, and spent a good four hours photographing them. As the tide came in and their stomachs were full, the birds settled down to roost together at high tide.

I was still photographing them when, all of a sudden, the whole flock took to the air with a raptor in pursuit. The sky was full of birds whizzing around, flushed by what I had now identified as a young peregrine falcon. I managed to lock focus on the raptor through the cloud of white and black and take a few images. It was all over in a flash but was an encounter that will stay with me.

Blackcock Fighting at Spring Lek
Animal Behaviour

Neil McIntyre
Black grouse (*Lyrurus tetrix*)
North Perthshire, Scotland

Nikon Z 9 with Nikon 500mm f/5.6 PF lens. 500mm; 1/800th second; f/5.6; ISO 2,500.

After watching the lek site from a distance to establish the birds' positions, I then introduced my hide to try to capture some of this spectacular spring spectacle. On this morning, I was blessed with decent light that afforded me a fast enough shutter speed to capture this image of two blackcocks having a full-blown fight in front of my hide. This particular one in the sequence stood out, with the bird on the left caught in a proper kung fu pose, about to strike.

Looking Up to Mum
Animal Behaviour

Alex Witt
Red fox (*Vulpes vulpes*)
London, England

Canon 1D X with Canon EF 100-400mm f/4.5-5.6L II lens. 300mm; 1/400th second; f/5.6; ISO 2,500.

To my surprise, whilst walking through the cemetery, I spotted a vixen running across ahead of me with what appeared to be a cub in her mouth. I carefully made my way over to where she had taken the cub and was greeted with five tiny blue-eyed cubs.
I managed to hide myself away and was privileged to witness and capture some very special playful, tender and intimate moments between the devoted mum and her young cubs.

Sitting Amongst the Locals
Animal Portraits

Rosie Barrett
Red fox (*Vulpes vulpes*)
Essex, England

Canon R7 with Canon EF 70-200mm f/2.8L II lens. 70mm; 1/1,250th second; f/4.5; ISO 800.

I've been photographing foxes for a few years, but none have ever been as curious and confident as this female fox in my local park. I lay low as she watched people from afar, waiting for them to drop scraps. Despite it being our first encounter, she bowled towards me and sat down, seemingly interested in what I was doing. She looked straight down my lens, creating a really unique moment between us. For that reason, it's one of my favourite photos of a fox, as I love getting down to the same level if I can, without causing disturbance.

Beauty and the Beast
Black & White

Andy Parkinson
Mute swan (*Cygnus olor*)
Derbyshire, England

Nikon Z 9 with Nikon Z 400mm f/2.8 lens.
400mm; 1/4,000th second; f/4.5; ISO 200.

I have photographed at the small lake local to me for some 15 years now, and every day I see something new. The swans that hold territory on this lake have always been ferociously territorial, but they seem to save a special ire for the arrival of any Canada goose. What is bad news for the Canada geese is usually good news for me, as this male will frequently set off in pursuit, as he did one evening, backlit by the late light.

Grey Seal Hunting Garfish
Coast & Marine

Robin Morrison
Grey seal (*Halichoerus grypus*)
Start Point, Devon, England

Canon R7 with Canon EF 500mm f/4L II lens. 500mm; 1/3,200th second; f/4; ISO 500.

From Start Point in Devon, I was watching tuna chasing a shoal of garfish when I noticed that the garfish were heading for the safety of a small, shallow cove below me. Unfortunately, there were a couple of grey seals already in the cove. These seals took advantage of the situation and started to chase down the garfish. The clear water and sandy bottom of the cove provided the perfect opportunity to watch the seals in action as the garfish tried to escape by leaping out of the water. Holding the camera to look vertically down was a real challenge.

Grey Seals Fighting
Animal Behaviour

Michael Watson
Grey seal (*Halichoerus grypus*)
Lincolnshire, England

Canon 1D X with Canon EF 500mm f/4L II lens and 1.4x teleconverter. 700mm; 1/1,250th second; f/5.6; ISO 1,600.

I've been taking pictures of Atlantic grey seals for over 12 years. This picture was taken at Donna Nook in Lincolnshire. The key is to make sure the tides are right and to be able to get close to the seals without disturbing them. Each trip has allowed me to observe their behaviour, and on this occasion two female seals engaged in some aggression, which only lasted a short while, as the tides drove the other seals towards them. Neither was badly injured, but getting this close took a lot of time crawling across the sand with very heavy gear.

Grappling
Coast & Marine

Philip Selby
Grey seal (*Halichoerus grypus*)
Horsey Gap, Norfolk, England

Canon R3 with Canon EF 300mm f/2.8L II lens and 2x teleconverter. 600mm; 1/1,250th second; f/5.6; ISO 2,500.

During an early autumn trip to Norfolk, I headed to Horsey Gap, home to one of the largest grey seal colonies in the UK. The pupping season had yet to begin, but there were numerous juvenile seals socialising and play fighting along the water's edge, providing great photographic opportunities. With my camera as close to the sand as possible, I was able to capture these two teeth-bearing individuals grappling in the surf.

Moon on a Sunny Day
Coast & Marine | Highly Commended

Billy Arthur
Moon jellyfish (*Aurelia aurita*)
Shetland Islands, Scotland

Sony A7R III with Sigma 15mm f/2.8 Fisheye lens. 15mm; 1/125th second; f/11; ISO 400.

Moon jellyfish arriving is a sign that summer is on its way. I had to wait for the sun to hide behind the clouds to avoid an overexposed sky. It was tricky to get the split just right, but after multiple shots I was happy with this one.

Fungi Textures
Botanical Britain

Paul Saunders
Fungus
Cambridge, England

Canon 5D Mark IV with Canon EF 100mm f/2.8L Macro lens. 100mm; 1/200th second; f/4; ISO 3,200.

I love looking for patterns and textures in my photography and this is one of the reasons I love photographing fungi so much. There are always so many interesting ways of photographing them and so many different views you can get. I found this group of mushrooms and wanted to get a close-up photo of their gills. I used two light panels to illuminate the gills fully and took a stack of 47 photos, as I was so close to the caps that my macro lens had a very short depth of field. It was a lot of work, but I love the lines that intertwine across the photo, with the caps of the fungi almost looking like rolling waves across the picture.

Evening Run
Animal Portraits

Kevin Sawford
European rabbit (*Oryctolagus cuniculus*)
Suffolk, England

Canon 1D X Mark II with Canon EF 500mm f/4L lens and 1.4x teleconverter. 700mm; 1/3,200th second; f/5.6; ISO 800.

A young rabbit runs across an area of grassland as the day's last rays of light create this backlit image. I captured this image at a local nature reserve where the rabbits are reasonably tolerant of humans but still need a good degree of fieldcraft to get close to them. Seeing the opportunity, I deliberately underexposed the image to get the rim lighting against the dark background as the rabbit ran over the grass.

On the Run
Black & White

Gordon Roach
Mountain hare (*Lepus timidus*)
Findhorn Valley, Scotland

Canon 5D Mark IV with Sigma 150-600mm f/5-6.3 Sports lens. 569mm; 1/2,500th second; f/8; ISO 640.

A mid-afternoon in January meant the sun was very low in the sky and facing me. The mountain hares weren't very active until this one stood and started running across the hillside in front of me, allowing me to capture the direct sun backlighting both the hare and the moving spindrift. I decided to change it to black and white to emphasise the contrasting light better.

The Smoking Roar
Animal Portraits

Takaki Nemoto
Red deer (*Cervus elaphus*)
London, England

Sony a9 II with Sony FE 600mm f/4 GM lens. 600mm; 1/1,600th second; f/4.5; ISO 100.

Cold, damp and invariably dark, there's nothing to wake up for before dawn in October. What kept me going, however, was the faint promise of a rutting photo where all the fickle variables might miraculously converge if I kept on trying as many times as I could.

Although I didn't have any clear vision of what the image should look like, I longed for an image that would take the viewer straight into the scene of the rut. How could I capture the thunderous bellows, the sharp morning chill and the smell of dead bracken mixed with the pheromone-packed urine from the stags in a single frame? As that thought rambled through my mind, a stag appeared from a nearby bush and started to bellow, irritated at the competition invisible to me. I lowered myself as close to the ground as possible and aimed my lens. As soon as it fired its furious roar towards the competition, the stag paused, leaving behind a trail of a long exhale mirroring the exact length of his bellow, crystallised in the morning light.

Redshank at Sunrise
Animal Portraits

James Roddie
Redshank (*Tringa totanus*)
North Uist, Outer Hebrides, Scotland

Nikon Z 9 with Nikon 500mm f/4 lens and 1.4x teleconverter. 700mm; 1/1,600th second; f/5.6; ISO 125.

After days of thick cloud and rain, a clear and bright dawn was forecast on North Uist. I set an early alarm and was out driving by 4:30am. I was mainly looking for short-eared owls, but there were plenty of other birds out and about as well. A bank of cloud on the horizon thankfully cleared just around sunrise, so it was clear there were going to be some beautiful conditions for photography. Luck was on my side when I came across this redshank perched perfectly against the light of the sunrise.

Golden Grass
Habitat

David Gibbon
Barn owl (*Tyto alba*)
Northumberland, England

Canon R3 with Canon EF 500mm f/4L II lens and 2x teleconverter. 1,000mm; 1/3,200th second; f/8; ISO 1,600.

There is an area in Northumberland that attracts barn owls and it's a place I often visit to photograph them. The location is perfect, allowing for some wonderfully backlit images. On this particular morning, I arrived before sunrise and saw a barn owl out hunting. As the sun rose above a hill behind the owl, it landed on this fence post. As I was using my 500mm lens and a 2x converter, this blew out the dew-covered grass and the beautiful morning sunrise turned it into a sea of golden, sparkling bokeh. The sun also created rim light around the barn owl, allowing me to create one of my favourite ever barn owl images.

Slime Mould
Botanical Britain

Andy Sands
Slime mould (*Lamproderma scintillans*)
Buckinghamshire, England

OM System OM-1 with OM 90mm f/3.5 lens and 2x teleconverter. 180mm; 1/8th second; f/16; ISO 200.

These wonderful, iridescent slime mould sporangia are growing on a decaying bracken frond; they are 1mm tall. A total of 37 images were taken in the field in natural light and were later focus stacked to create the final image.

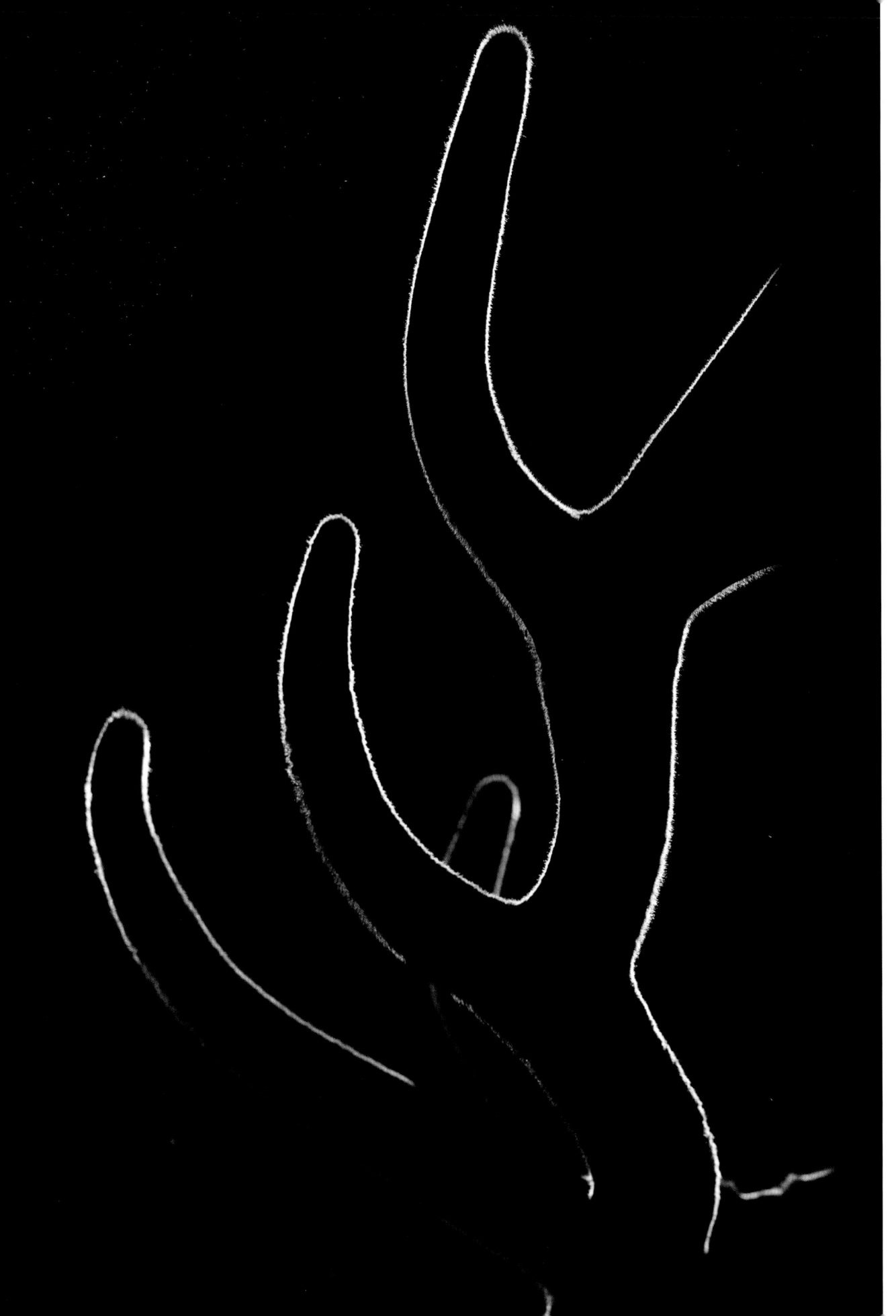

Velvet Outline
Black & White

Matthew Cattell
Red deer (*Cervus elaphus*)
Bushy Park, Surrey, England

Nikon Z 9 with Nikon 500mm f/4 lens. 500mm; 1/1,250th second; f/8; ISO 400.

I like to visit the red deer in the London parks throughout the year, and on this particular morning, I found a large male resting on the edge of some woodland. Being early summer, his antlers were covered in velvet and the small hairs and fibres were catching the morning sun. I positioned my camera so that the backlit antlers could be captured against a dark background. Then, exposing for the highlights, I explored the resulting curves and lines to create a series of abstract images.

Golden Hour
Habitat

Bret Charman
Roe deer (*Capreolus capreolus*)
South Downs National Park, Hampshire, England

Canon 1D X Mark II with Canon EF 500mm f/4L II lens. 500mm; 1/2,500th second; f/4; ISO 1,000.

The roe deer is arguably the most widespread of the deer species that inhabit the UK. However, it is in the patchwork of farmers' fields and woods that they are found at their highest densities. I've been photographing them for many years, but trying to capture backlit images is never easy. I saw this buck appear on the edge of a thicket, and he slowly ventured out into the field margin, where the setting sun illuminated him as he carefully picked his route. I wanted to keep the detail and the atmosphere, so I carefully adjusted my exposure to suit, underexposing slightly to capture the feel of the scene that lay before me.

On the Monet
Wild Woods | Highly Commended

Paul Goldstein
Bluebells (*Hyacinthoides non-scripta*)
Westerham, England

Canon 1D X Mark III with Canon EF 70-200mm f/2.8L II lens. 95mm; 1/6th second; f/13; ISO 125.

Every spring, I try different ways to photograph bluebells; the combination of fresh beech leaves and new purple flowers with their Wimbledon tennis livery is intoxicating enough to lure me to Kent and Surrey woodlands.

A short walk near the two counties' border led me to something I had waited years to find: the combination of early flowers with a rape field beyond. I tried many experiments, all of them predictable and uninspiring record shots. Handholding and moving the camera up and down at a ridiculously low speed was a more ambitious policy but finally produced something different. I have always liked slow shutter speeds with any subject, mainly because no one shot is ever the same.

Bluebell Wood
Wild Woods

Ian Wade
Bluebells (*Hyacinthoides non-scripta*)
Somerset, England

Canon 5D Mark II with Canon EF 17-40mm f/4L lens.
17mm; 1/30th second; f/7.1; ISO 500.

Photographing bluebells whilst lying on the ground and looking up created a really interesting image of blurred flowers in the foreground with the tree canopy in the distance.

Oystercatchers in the Shallows
Coast & Marine

David Shawe
Oystercatcher (*Haematopus ostralegus*)
Luskentyre, Isle of Harris, Scotland

Canon R5 with Canon RF 100-500mm f/4.5-7.1L lens. 500mm; 1/1,600th second; f/7.1; ISO 640.

Whilst on a landscape photography trip to Lewis and Harris, these oystercatchers at Luskentyre caught my eye for ages, with their random left-right and up-down movements. The colourful sea and waves behind them gave a sense of place and scale, with the colours making a striking contrast to the black-and-white bodies of the birds. To prevent scaring them off, I stayed by the dunes at the back of the beach and used a 500mm lens, the additional benefit being the compression of the scene to add a touch of drama.

Otterly Beautiful
Animal Portraits | Highly Commended

Marc Freebrey
Otter (*Lutra lutra*)
Gloucestershire Canal, England

Nikon Z 9 with NIkon Z 180-600mm f/5.6-6.3 lens. 400mm; 1/1,000th second; f/6.3; ISO 2,000.

I often walk the Stroud Waters Canal to take photographs of local wildlife. The otters were active, with two young pups to feed, so there was extra feeding activity. There is one spot under the viaduct where you can get to water/eye level. I was enjoying watching the otter chase fish and was lucky enough to be in place as the mother came past, clearly very secure in her environment and unconcerned by my presence, so much so that she popped up close by and splashed water at me.

Rustic Crossing
Wild Woods

Max Ellis
Red deer (*Cervus elaphus*)
London, England

Nikon D5 with Nikon 70-200mm f/2.8 lens. 70mm; 1/320th second; f/4.5; ISO 400.

On this day, I'd woken up later than I intended, cross with myself for missing so much of the wonderful autumn light. I made my way to this quiet clearing in the woods and sat down, thinking I'll just wait here until something really wonderful happens. I was quite prepared to sit there all day and night if necessary, but after only about 10 minutes, as if by magic, I heard a rustle, and this majestic stag ambled out precisely where I visualised and took a leisurely stroll through this perfect rustic scene.

Fairy Night Light
Botanical Britain

Roy McDonald
Parachute fungus (*Marasmius rotula*)
Ashridge Woods, England

Nikon Z 6 II with Nikon 300mm f/4 lens. 300mm; 1/1,600th second; f/4; ISO 1,600.

For the past few years, I've been refining a technique: using a torch to illuminate fungi in the darkness of the woodland. While most fungi grow on the forest floor, this parachute fungus occasionally sprouts high in the trees, making photography challenging. For this shot, I stumbled upon an isolated tiny fungus and used a GorillaPod wrapped around a tree branch to hold the camera, a task that required patience and effort. By linking my camera to my mobile phone, I could stand on tiptoes and hold the torch above the fungus. After numerous attempts, I finally achieved the effect I was after, turning a small fungus into a woodland fairy night light.

Feeding Time
Animal Behaviour

James Roddie
Short-eared owl (*Asio flammeus*)
North Uist, Scotland

Nikon Z 9 with Nikon 500mm f/4 lens and 1.4x teleconverter. 700mm; 1/1,250th second; f/5.6; ISO 320.

Mid-summer is a great time to spot short-eared owl fledglings in the Outer Hebrides. I had been driving my car along a single-track road when I saw a young owl sitting on a fence some distance away. I pulled up and fixed a 1.4x teleconverter to my 500mm lens. The fledgling started to flap and hiss, looking at something in the distance. I instinctively started to take photos, and my heart raced as another owl appeared in the frame carrying a dead rodent. It was a parent bringing food for its fledgling. The entire encounter lasted seconds.

Enjoy the Silence
Animal Portraits

Norman Watson
Short-eared owl (*Asio flammeus*)
Aberdeenshire, Scotland

Canon R5 with Canon EF 400mm f/2.8L II lens and 1.4x teleconverter. 560mm; 1/1,000th second; f/2.8; ISO 3,200.

It doesn't get much better than photographing an owl hunting. Sitting hidden against a grassy bank, I'd just set up my camera when this short-eared owl appeared, hanging on the gentlest breeze across the grassland. No noise, staying airborne with minimal effort on broad wings, listening for the faintest sound – these owls are masters at hunting rodents. It could probably hear my heart thumping as it flew closer to me!

Leveret on the Run
Animal Portraits

Alastair Marsh
Brown hare (*Lepus europaeus*)
North Yorkshire, England

Canon R3 with Canon EF 500mm f/4L lens.
500mm; 1/1,600th second; f/4; ISO 1,000.

Each spring, I spend as much time watching a good population of hares local to me. In 2023, I had my best season to date. They would regularly use this farm track to cross from field to field. This leveret was the star of my time with the hares last year. It would regularly appear out of nowhere and bound around in a childlike way, which was so entertaining to watch. On this occasion, it came zooming towards me, and with this one frame I was able to get it completely off the ground.

Rabbit
Habitat

Chris Hawes
European rabbit (*Oryctolagus cuniculus*)
Cardiff, Wales

Canon 1D X Mark II with Canon EF 300mm f/2.8L II lens and 2x teleconverter. 600mm; 1/800th second; f/5.6; ISO 800.

One spring, I set myself the challenge of photographing the young rabbits amongst wildflowers at the local nature reserve. There was a small window of a few weeks when the flowers were out and the vegetation was short enough to still see the rabbits, so I made several early morning visits during this period, trying to capture the images I had in mind. This image is backlit by the sun and shows a slightly older rabbit pausing for a break between feeding.

Common Sandpiper with Dragonfly
Animal Behaviour

Ian Mason
Common sandpiper (*Actitis hypoleucos*)
Perthshire, Scotland

Canon 1D X with Canon EF 600mm f/4L lens. 600mm; 1/1,250th second; f/4; ISO 1,600.

I was set up at the edge of a Perthshire loch to watch a sunset when I became aware of a solitary sandpiper strolling past at the waterline. Luckily, I had my long lens with me, so I set it up. The bird made several passes, seemingly oblivious to my presence. I was astonished to see it nonchalantly pick up a dragonfly from a nearby rock. I had no idea they ate these! I was interested and surprised to see the comparative sizes of the two species.

Dragonfl-eye
Animal Behaviour

James Ball
Eleonora's falcon (*Falco eleonorae*)
Kent, England

Canon 5D Mark IV with Canon EF 300mm f/2.8L II lens and 2x teleconverter. 600mm; 1/2,000th second; f/5.6; ISO 500.

Eleanora's falcon, a very rare visitor to these shores – this particular bird is thought to be the first ever photographed in the UK. It behaves similarly to the more commonly seen hobby, catching insects on the wing and migrating further north on the globe in summer. I observed the bird hawking insects in a nearby field as I stood on a pathway, using a hawthorn bush for some disguise. I was fortunate when it chose to dive down not too far away from me, about 25 metres, and then fly back up to reveal the dragonfly. At first, I was frustrated that the dragonfly covered the eye of the falcon, but on reflection I quite like that it shows the size of its meal and, if you look close enough, you can see the bird's eye through the delicate wing.

Rough and Tumble
Animal Behaviour

James Yaxley
Stoat (*Mustela erminea*)
Strumpshaw Fen, Norfolk, England

Canon R5 with Canon EF 500mm f/4L II lens and 1.4x teleconverter. 700mm; 1/2,500th second; f/5.6; ISO 6,400.

I was at my local nature reserve early one morning in July when I saw some movement in the grass. On closer inspection, I was delighted to discover it was a female stoat play fighting with its offspring. The action was frantic as the stoats wrestled with each other, leaping and pouncing in a breathtaking performance of speed and agility. The unpredictable and erratic nature of their rough and tumble made capturing a decent image very challenging. This image is the best of the action shots, with the young stoat attacking its mother, its razor-sharp teeth on display.

Pine Marten Duo
Animal Portraits

Alastair Marsh
Pine marten (*Martes martes*)
Ardnamurchan, Scotland

Canon R3 with Canon EF 300mm f/2.8L lens. 300mm; 1/800th second; f/2.8; ISO 1,600.

I spend as much time as possible each summer in the Highlands to see pine martens. In July, I spent a couple of weeks in Ardnamurchan, where I was fortunate enough to watch these amazing animals each evening as they visited the cottage I was staying at. They were tempted by some peanuts and raisins I left out each night. Seeing Mum and her kit together like this, especially with the heather in the garden in flower, was the icing on the cake.

Great Crested Grebe with a Trail of Gold
Animal Portraits

Richard Sheldrake
Great crested grebe (*Podiceps cristatus*)
Lakeside, Eastleigh, England

Nikon Z 9 with Nikon Z 400mm f/2.8 lens and 1.4x teleconverter. 560mm; 1/2,500th second; f/4; ISO 1,600.

I was low on the bank of the lake, watching the grebe and desperately hoping it would swim through this amazing patch of dappled sunlight which shone through the trees momentarily. On this occasion, it did what I wanted and swam right through the light. Photography is all about angles and light; here, everything just came together, lying on the muddy bank to get the low angle and the dappled light in exactly the right place.

Fishing for Breakfast
Black & White | Highly Commended

Steve Palmer
Great crested grebe (*Podiceps cristatus*)
Black Lake, Lindow Common, Wilmslow, Cheshire, England

Pentax K1 with Pentax 300mm f/4 lens. 300mm; 1/400th second; f/5.6; ISO 200.

As the early morning sun rises, its light threads its way through the bare trees on the east side of the lake, creating pools of light and shadow. The local great crested grebe likes to hunt for its breakfast on that side. Each time it dived, I waited patiently for it to resurface in one of the pools of light.

Knots Landing
Black & White

Deborah Hockey
Knot (*Calidris canutus*)
Snettisham Nature Reserve, England

Sony a1 with Sony FE 200-600mm f/5.6-6.3 G lens. 600mm; 1/40th second; f/18; ISO 400.

Before the tens of thousands of waders who have gathered in the lagoon take off to go and feed on the mudflats, there's a constant ebb and flow of birds leaving and joining the flock. By dropping my shutter speed to 1/40 sec, I was able to convey the fluidity of the movement of these birds in contrast to those who were standing still. No matter how tightly packed together the flock was, they always seemed to find a place to land!

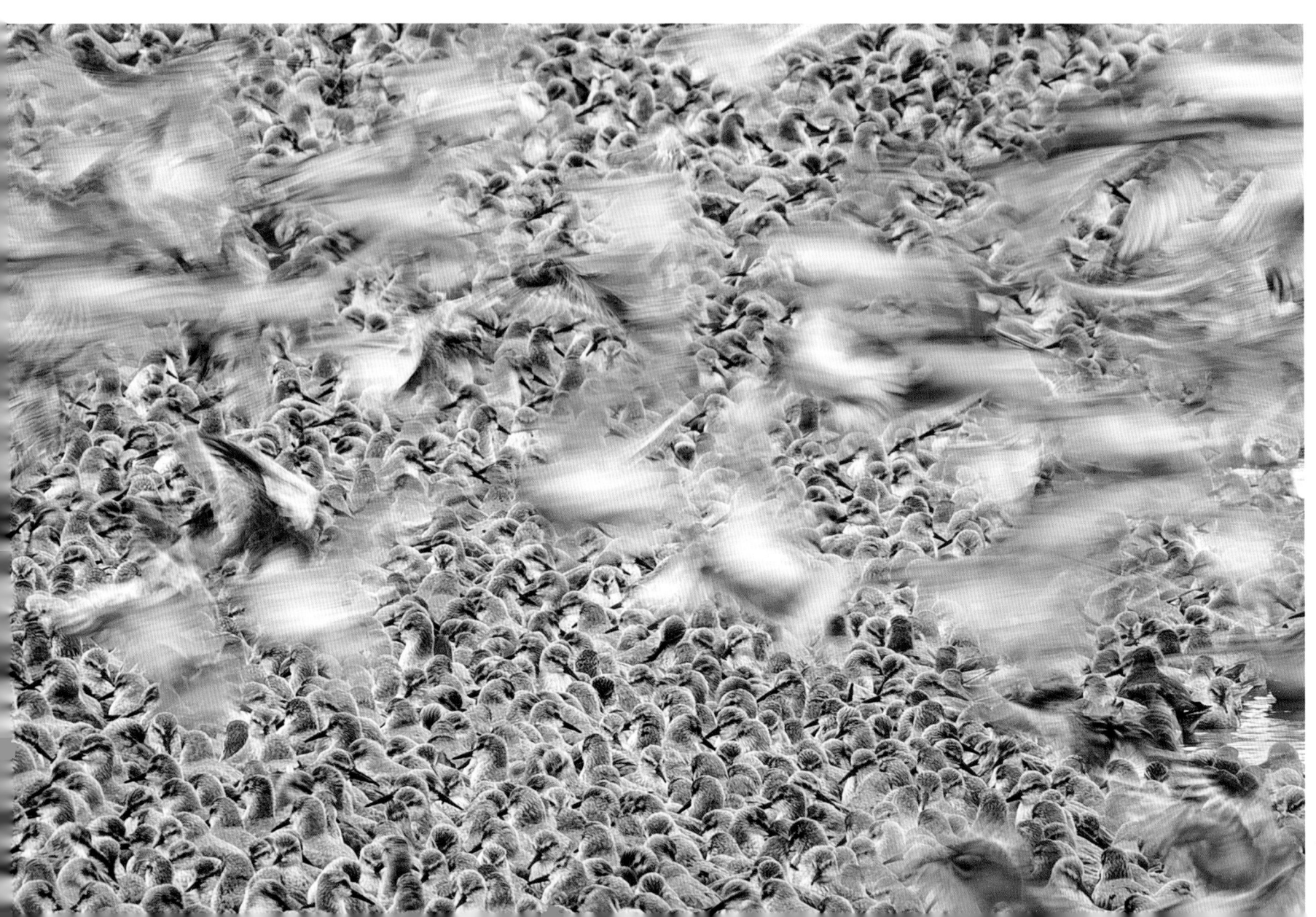

Roosting Dragons
Hidden Britain | Winner

Daniel Trim
Broad-bodied chaser (*Libellula depressa*)
Ham Wall, England

Canon 5DS with Canon EF 70-200mm f/2.8L II lens. 200mm; 1/1,600th second; f/2.8; ISO 800.

Each year in May, there is a huge emergence of dragonflies at RSPB Ham Wall, and if you're there early enough you can see them all roosting in the reeds in impressive groups. This group was climbing the reeds, ready to warm up once the sun came above the horizon. I've used an in-camera double exposure, with one frame sharp on the subject and one with a soft focus for an ethereal feel.

Mother's Milk
Animal Behaviour

Daniel Trim
Wild boar (*Sus scrofa*)
Forest of Dean, England

Canon 5DS with Canon EF 500mm f/4L II lens. 500mm; 1/125th second; f/4; ISO 1,000.

After watching a very active sounder of humbugs for over an hour, they all settled down and started to feed. Getting the right angle was tricky, but at the point when the mother had enough, she stood up, shaking most of them away yet allowing this one to feed for a short while longer in clear view. I took my chance!

Private Moment
Animal Behaviour | Highly Commended

Sarah Darnell
Brown hare (*Lepus europaeus*)
Norfolk, England

Canon 1D X Mark II with Canon EF 600mm f/4L II lens and 1.4x teleconverter. 840mm; 1/2,000th second; f/5.6; ISO 1,250.

I spend a lot of time out in my local Norfolk fields photographing hares. Sometimes, I am lucky enough to witness the chasing, dancing and prancing of the courtship process. This pair of hares stayed close to each other, eating, preening and cuddling up, leading to the moment when they sealed the deal in front of me. This was the first time I had witnessed such behaviour, so I was fascinated and at the same time felt a little awkward being present at this intimate moment. It was surprisingly calm, but an intense connection. A true privilege to watch the next generation of beautiful hares begin.

White Wings on Black Cliffs
Black & White

Jane Hope
Northern fulmar (*Fulmarus glacialis*)
Handa Island, Scotland

Canon R3 with Canon RF 100-500mm f/4.5-7.1L lens. 500mm; 1/2,500th second; f/8; ISO 1,000.

Fulmars typically glide back and forth along their breeding cliffs with stiff wings. On this occasion, there was a strong sun catching the bright white birds against black cliffs that were thrown into shadow. It was this contrast that attracted me to the photograph. It required exposure compensation of -2.7 to keep the white bird properly exposed.

The Seal Cave
Coast & Marine | Runner-up

Ben Porter
Grey seal (*Halichoerus grypus*)
Bardsey Island, Wales

Canon 6D with Canon EF 16-35mm f/4L lens.
19mm; 1/60th second; f/4.5; ISO 2,000.

A young grey seal breaks the surface in the clear turquoise waters of a coastal cave on Bardsey Island, North Wales. This cave sees up to 30 or more seals hauling out within its depths, entering and exiting via a secret seaward passage beneath the waters. Sitting quietly above gives an amazing opportunity to watch their comings and goings, their behaviours and to hear their remarkable vocalisations at close quarters. Sometimes, the elements of light, tide and the behaviour of the seals collide to provide an image like this – one of my favourites from my visits to this remarkable site.

Angel of the Morning
Black & White

Lee O'Dwyer
Long-tailed tit (*Aegithalos caudatus*)
Lytham, Lancashire, England

OM System OM-1 with OM 40-150mm f/2.8 lens and 1.4x teleconverter. 210mm; 1/4,000th second; f/5.6; ISO 1,000.

This image was created at my garden setup for small birds in flight. I have a selection of feeders that attract various species, including my favourites, long-tailed tits. In the winter months, I have a window of about one and a half hours when, on a cloudless day, the sun rises in just the right position to capture this beautiful backlight in the bird's wings. This was one such day and one of the rare occasions when it all came together. The position of the bird, the light and the element of luck that is always needed rewarded my patience. For every successful image, there are many near misses and always something new to be learned for the next time.

Pink & Blue
Animal Portraits

Drew Buckley
Oystercatcher (*Haematopus ostralegus*)
Skomer Island, Pembrokeshire, Wales

Canon EOS R5, EF500mm f/4L IS II USM.

While the puffins are the stars of the show on Skomer Island, there's plenty of other wildlife to keep me interested too. During May, the island is awash with colourful wildflowers like bluebells and red campion. Here, a roosting oystercatcher on a stone wall is framed by getting down low and shooting through the flowers, using a shallow aperture to isolate the bird against the sea behind.

Wasp Nest and Golden Flight Trails
Hidden Britain

Andrew Bailey
Common wasps (*Vespula vulgaris*)
Suffolk, England

Nikon D850 with Nikon 200-400mm f/4 lens. 280mm; 1/6th second; f/32; ISO 400.

Common wasps took up residence in a nest box under the eaves of the log cabin in our garden. During the building phase of the nest, they started by papering over the majority of the box before beginning to build a dome from the underside of the bird box. The nest was extremely active in this early stage, and when disturbed the wasps would fly around the nest, mounting an airborne defence of their home. This photo shows the frenzy of activity, with the wasps flying around, lit by strong sunshine, while the nest under the eaves of the log cabin remains in shadow beyond. The activity subsided quickly when no threat was detected. I used a long exposure to try to capture the flight paths of the wasps and fired pulses of flash during the exposure, aiming to partially freeze the activity of some wasps whilst retaining some of the feeling of movement in the image. The golden colour of the wasps as they circle the nest acts as a warning and the cumulative effect of the number of wasps involved helps to deter potential predators.

Bus Pass
Urban Wildlife | Runner-up

Paul Goldstein
Swan (*Cygnus olor*)
Mitcham, England

Canon 1D X Mark II with Canon EF 100-400mm f/4.5-5.6L II lens. 300mm; 1/20th second; f/5.6; ISO 100.

A small South London pond is a perfect yet perhaps incongruous venue for a swan study. A pair has nested there for many years, and in spring they successfully raised cygnets. The cob reigned over the water like a medieval baron, vanquishing all but the ducks. Geese of several descriptions and even crows were sent packing. Sometimes, he would wander onto the main London road and hold up traffic. Often, he would keep watch over his family inches from the cars and lorries. To try to portray this urban avian family meant a very early start and actually standing in the deep mud in the middle of the pond before the fountain went on with a tripod, long lens, two-second delay, slow shutter speed, oh, and a bus.

Grouse Lekking
Animal Portraits

Saleel Tambe
Black grouse (*Lyrurus tetrix*)
Perthshire, Scotland

Sony a1 with Sony FE 200-600mm f/5.6-6.3 G lens. 303mm; 1/1,000th second; f/6.3; ISO 3,200.

The black grouse display a very unique courtship phenomenon called lekking. There are certain fixed spots called leks deep inside the woods or on mountain slope heathlands. During this courtship period, the males start gathering here in the early hours before sunrise. With a bubbling sound, they try to display their dominance over each other to win the females. This lekking occurs only for a week or two during the whole year. The early morning light (in fact, darkness) makes photography very challenging and capturing any action is a tough task. I managed to capture two contending males just before sunrise.

Territorial Dispute
Coast & Marine

Michael van Wegen
Grey seal (*Halichoerus grypus*)
Horsey Gap, England

Canon 1D X Mark II with Canon EF 600mm f/4L II lens and 1.4x teleconverter. 840mm; 1/1,600th second; f/13; ISO 6,400.

During autumn, grey seals come ashore on British beaches for the birth of their pups. While the females are giving birth and suckling the pups, the males start to establish territory to be present when the females become receptive to mating after the pups have been weaned. These two males intended to control the same area of the beach, resulting in a tussle. The UK is a stronghold for grey seals, with about 35-40% of the global population living in British waters. The Norfolk colonies on the English east coast have shown strong growth over the past decade, now representing some of the largest grey seal colonies in the UK. Although this is a great success story, the Norfolk coast faces erosion, which is accelerated by increased storm activity as a result of climate change. This is a real threat to the beach and dune areas where the grey seals come ashore to give birth to their pups in November and December.

Buffet Time
Animal Portraits

Tom Kelly
White-throated dipper (*Cinclus cinclus*)
Edinburgh, Scotland

Nikon Z 9 with Sigma 150-600mm f/5-6.3 lens. 600mm; 1/800th second; f/6.3; ISO 2,200.

The peaty colour of the water and the shade from the trees created a dark atmosphere that framed this dipper as a slither of sunlight caught it full on. But there was something else that caught my attention. Normally, it's all fast-moving, water-splashing and non-stop action as they forage at their free-for-all buffet, but not on this occasion. There was an element of serenity about this dipper as it slowly and delicately fed itself in this ethereal moment.

Common Sandpiper in the Rapids
Animal Portraits

Jonathan Gaunt
Common sandpiper (*Actitis hypoleucos*)
North Northumberland, England

Canon R6 with Canon RF 100-500mm f/4.5-7.1L lens. 451mm; 1/25th second; f/6.3; ISO 100.

Common sandpipers are summer migrants and visit this Northumbrian upland river, usually arriving in mid-April each year to breed. I set up a temporary low-level hide as close to the river's edge as possible. My aim was to photograph the bird using a very low shutter speed to try to blur the fast-moving water while also getting the bird as sharp as possible. This was made more challenging as sandpipers are rarely still, constantly bobbing up and down as they snatch insects from the river as they float past.

Early Morning Thrift
Coast & Marine

Mike Tibbotts
Sea thrift (*Armeria maritima*)
Dumfries, Scotland

Nikon Z 8 with Nikon Z 180-600mm f/5.6-6.3 lens. 180mm; 1/500th second; f/8; ISO 220.

Thrift, a colourful coastal plant, is often seen growing near the shoreline around our coasts and is seen here on the lichen-covered rocks on the Solway Firth. This shot was captured just after daybreak, with the rising sun nicely backlighting the stems.

Puffin Sundowner
Animal Portraits

Richard Peters
Atlantic puffin (*Fratercula arctica*)
Skomer Island, Pembrokeshire, Wales

Nikon Z 9 with Nikon Z 70-200mm f/2.8 lens. 180mm; 1/2,000th second; f/5.6; ISO 125.

With just minutes to go, and with me sitting in place, waiting patiently, a puffin walked into the perfect spot to be framed alongside the setting sun on Skomer Island. Although puffins don't 'call', this one stretched its neck out and opened its beak as if to display its typical yawning behaviour. Framed against the sun, it was the perfect pose for the scene.

Snipe Alights
Animal Portraits

Martin Vaughan
Common snipe (*Gallinago gallinago*)
Near Ibstock, Leicestershire, England

Canon 1D X with Canon EF 500mm f/4L lens and 1.4x teleconverter. 700mm; 1/4,000th second; f/5.6; ISO 1,250.

At a local Wildlife Trust reserve, I had permission to have a small temporary hide among the reeds so I could shoot at water level. Occasionally, snipe will come and bathe and preen, but they are very shy about leaving the safety of the reeds. One was in a patch of morning sun, so I focused on it, wondering if it would bathe when it took off. I caught it with the trail of water streaming off its legs. I thought it characterised the flighty nature of the species, which is so easily startled and takes wing.

Dipper
Habitat

Chris Hawes
White-throated dipper (*Cinclus cinclus*)
Kinross, Scotland

Canon 1D X Mark II with Canon EF 300mm f/2.8L II lens and 2x teleconverter. 600mm; 1/640th second; f/8; ISO 1,600.

For the last couple of years, I've photographed a pair of dippers as they successfully nested and raised their young on a local river. They've treated me to a number of lovely encounters and enabled me to capture images I'm pleased with. On this occasion, I photographed downstream into the light, which caused the spray created by the cascading water to be backlit against the dark background. I thought this created an interesting effect and was grateful when one of the dipper pair obligingly appeared on this rock, framing itself with the backlit droplets of water.

Hedgehog Reflections
Animal Behaviour

Alastair Marsh
Hedgehog (*Erinaceus europaeus*)
North Yorkshire, England

Canon R3 with Canon EF 300mm f/2.8L lens. 300mm; 1/640th second; f/3.5; ISO 1,600.

Having dug a pond in our garden a few years ago, we now get all kinds of wildlife visitors. Above all, our favourite are the evening visits from hedgehogs. We're lucky to get nightly visits from three and occasionally four hedgehogs now. They come for the food we leave out each night, as well as for a drink at the edge of the pond. If I'm lucky, this hedgehog will appear just before it gets dark, allowing me to take images like this. Turning our garden into a 'wildlife garden' was one of the best things we've done.

Hedgehog Silhouette
Habitat

Wendy Ball
Hedgehog (*Erinaceus europaeus*)
During the night in my garden

Canon 5D Mark III with Canon EF 100mm f/2.8 Macro lens. 100mm; 1/125th second; f/8; ISO 640.

Camera trapping is notoriously frustrating and time consuming, with many, many failures. Trying to obtain this image was no exception. With the aid of trail cameras, I knew that throughout the summer three hedgehogs were regular visitors to our garden. One of their favourite places was along this path, where they would hunt for the slugs that emerged after dark from their hiding places among the daisies and between the paving stones. I was able to identify and gain an intimate knowledge of the individuals and understand their behaviour and patterns of visiting.

This knowledge enabled me to place my camera and flash units without disturbing or altering their behaviour. I tried a variety of techniques, using one to three flash units with an automatic trigger and the camera set overnight in a waterproof housing, pre-focused and using silent mode. Everything had to be pre-planned and set accurately, as I would be in bed asleep. A considerable amount of knowledgeable finesse was required to be creative in my deployment of the flash units. My aim was to subtly backlight the hedgehog, with no distractions, against the lovely backdrop of the daisies.

Short-eared Owl
Animal Behaviour

Ian Mason
Short-eared owl (*Asio flammeus*)
North Uist, Scotland

Canon 1D X with Canon EF 600mm f/4L lens.
600mm; 1/125th second; f/4; ISO 400.

I came across a family of short-eared owls close to the roadside in North Uist. They were quite confiding, and I was able to take several images from the car. This individual was particularly curious and turned its head a little every time the shutter clicked, until it appeared totally upside down! It takes some viewers a while to understand what they are seeing.

Choughing About
Animal Behaviour

Deborah Hockey
Chough (*Pyrrhocorax pyrrhocorax*)
Pembrokeshire, Wales

Sony a1 with Sony FE 200-600mm f/5.6-6.3 G lens. 600mm; 1/2,000th second; f/7.1; ISO 1,000.

I spent a week in Pembrokeshire hoping to get a chance to photograph the choughs at Stackpole Head. One evening, whilst walking along the cliffs, I saw these two juvenile birds seemingly playing while their parents scoured the grass for food. They were an absolute delight to watch as they tussled with each other, without a care in the world.

Strike a Pose
Animal Portraits

Rosalie Smith
Bearded reedling
(*Panurus biarmicus*)
Kent, England

Canon R5 with Canon EF 500mm f/4L II lens. 500mm; 1/1,000th second; f/4; ISO 1,250.

After months of no luck walking to a spot where bearded reedlings had been reported, I finally spotted a male flitting through the reeds. I was thrilled to have found one at last, but the challenge of photographing it was just beginning.
As anyone familiar with these birds knows, they're very skittish and don't linger for long. But then, my moment came – this bearded reedling paused briefly on the reeds, long enough for me to capture the shot before it flew off. I was ecstatic to have caught it in the classic pose between two reeds!

Streetlit Snowdrop
Botanical Britain | Winner

Jacob J. Watson-Howland
Snowdrop (*Galanthus nivalis*)
Canterbury, England

Canon R6 with Sigma 150-600mm f/5-6.3 Contemporary lens. 600mm; 3.2 seconds; f/6.3; ISO 160.

Galanthus nivalis, the snowdrop, defies winter's chill. Its adaptations, like producing proteins that act as natural antifreeze, allow them to survive sub-freezing temperatures. This botanical wonder thrives in woodlands, parks and urban environments. One of Britain's earliest blooms, its elegant form and modest flower signal the changing seasons. This image, taken under a city streetlight using a slow shutter speed, highlights snowdrop's unique adaptations to Britain's unpredictable and changing climate.

Magical Mandarin
Animal Portraits

Lauren McIntyre
Mandarin duck (*Aix galericulata*)
Bushy Park, London, England

Nikon D850 with Sigma 150-600mm f/5-6.3 Contemporary lens. 600mm; 1/1,250th second; f/6.3; ISO 1,250.

The last thing I expected to see while looking for bunnies in the woodland gardens was a mandarin in a patch of bluebells. I couldn't believe my luck: a male in its beautiful breeding plumage in the most stunning area. It was initially pecking around in the grass near the bluebells, so I took my position and waited, hoping it would wander over into them. I was delighted when it eventually did, and even more so when it looked up for a moment and fluffed up its head feathers as if posing for me. The perfect first encounter with this beautiful bird.

Cocktail – Male Blackbird
Animal Portraits

John Macfarlane
Blackbird (*Turdus merula*)
Cumbria, England

Canon R5 with Canon RF 100-500mm f/4.5-7.1 lens. 500mm; 1/400th second; f/7.1; ISO 1,000.

I was sitting in the garden, enjoying my first cup of coffee, as the March sun appeared over the nearby mountains, warming the scene. The air was alive with bird calls. A male blackbird flew down to perch on an old branch, shouting its alarm call – chik, chuk, chik, chuk – at a nearby rival. As it took off to confront the intruder, it did that characteristic cock of its tail, which caught the early sun's rays coming from the right, the rest of its body silhouetted against the darker shades of the mountains beyond. A common but beautiful bird.

◀ **Reflections**
Hidden Britain | Highly Commended

Rachel Piper
Spider (Arachnida)
Hemel Hempstead, Herts, England

Canon 7D Mark II with Canon EF 60mm f/2.8 Macro lens. 60mm; 1/160th second; f/3.5; ISO 800.

I photographed these water droplets on this spider's web as the sun returned to my garden, but I didn't see the full picture until I looked at it on my computer screen and saw reflections of a solitary tiny spider in each one. I love macro photography because it enables me to capture worlds that you would not normally see, and on this occasion I was not disappointed.

British Stars and Stripes
Coast & Marine

Jenny Stock
Brittle stars (Ophiuroidea)
Loch Leven, Scotland

Canon 5D Mark IV with Canon EF 100mm f/2.8L Macro lens. 100mm; 1/125th second; f/10; ISO 100.

As I descended into the dark green waters of Loch Leven on a dusk dive, I approached an area where my torch picked out the vivid colours of a living carpet of thousands of brittle stars, clustered together in a dense carpet on the seabed. Captivated by the variety of hues and patterns each star exhibited, I felt this was an incredible encounter with a unique species, and I was delighted with the bold graphic photo that the encounter yielded.

Night-time Wanderings
Urban Wildlife

James Roddie
Pine marten (*Martes martes*)
Near Inverness, Scotland

Nikon D750 with Nikon 16-35mm f/4 lens. 16mm; 1/200th second; f/10; ISO 1,600.

Pine martens will often visit abandoned buildings to hunt mice during the winter months, when other food is scarcer. After finding pine marten scat (droppings) in this derelict farm, I set up a trail camera and found that an individual pine marten was occasionally visiting to hunt. I decided to set up a DSLR camera trap in the building to try to capture some high-quality images. I used three flashes for lighting and a PIR sensor to trigger the camera. When I came back to check the camera after two days, I had dozens of photos of mice and a few images of the pine marten, of which this was the best.

Darter Dreaming Under the Milky Way
Hidden Britain | Highly Commended

Andrew Fusek Peters
Black darter (*Sympetrum danae*)
Shropshire, England

OM System OM-1 with OM 7-14mm f/2.8 lens. 8mm; 20 seconds; f/3.5; ISO 16,000.

I have spent 10 years photographing and studying the black darter dragonfly population on the Long Mynd as part of a long-term commission for the National Trust. During that time, I tried to work out how to capture a roosting dragonfly and the Milky Way in the same single raw exposure. The hard work finally paid off, and using a combination of foreground lighting and manual attachments to my lens, I was able to frame near and far, macro and cosmic, and perhaps reflect on the spirit of the place where the night is full of sleeping dragonflies and soaring stars.

Two Worlds
Coast & Marine

Gina Goodman
Compass jellyfish (*Chrysaora hysoscella*)
Falmouth, Cornwall, England

Canon R5 with Canon RF 15-35mm f/2.8L lens. 31mm; 1/320th second; f/10; ISO 125.

This image was taken by exploiting a phenomenon of light called Snell's window. When underwater and the light is at the correct angle, it's as though a porthole to the sky opens. For this image, I used a rectilinear lens to exclude the edges of the portal from the frame. This creates the illusion of a sky-bound jellyfish.

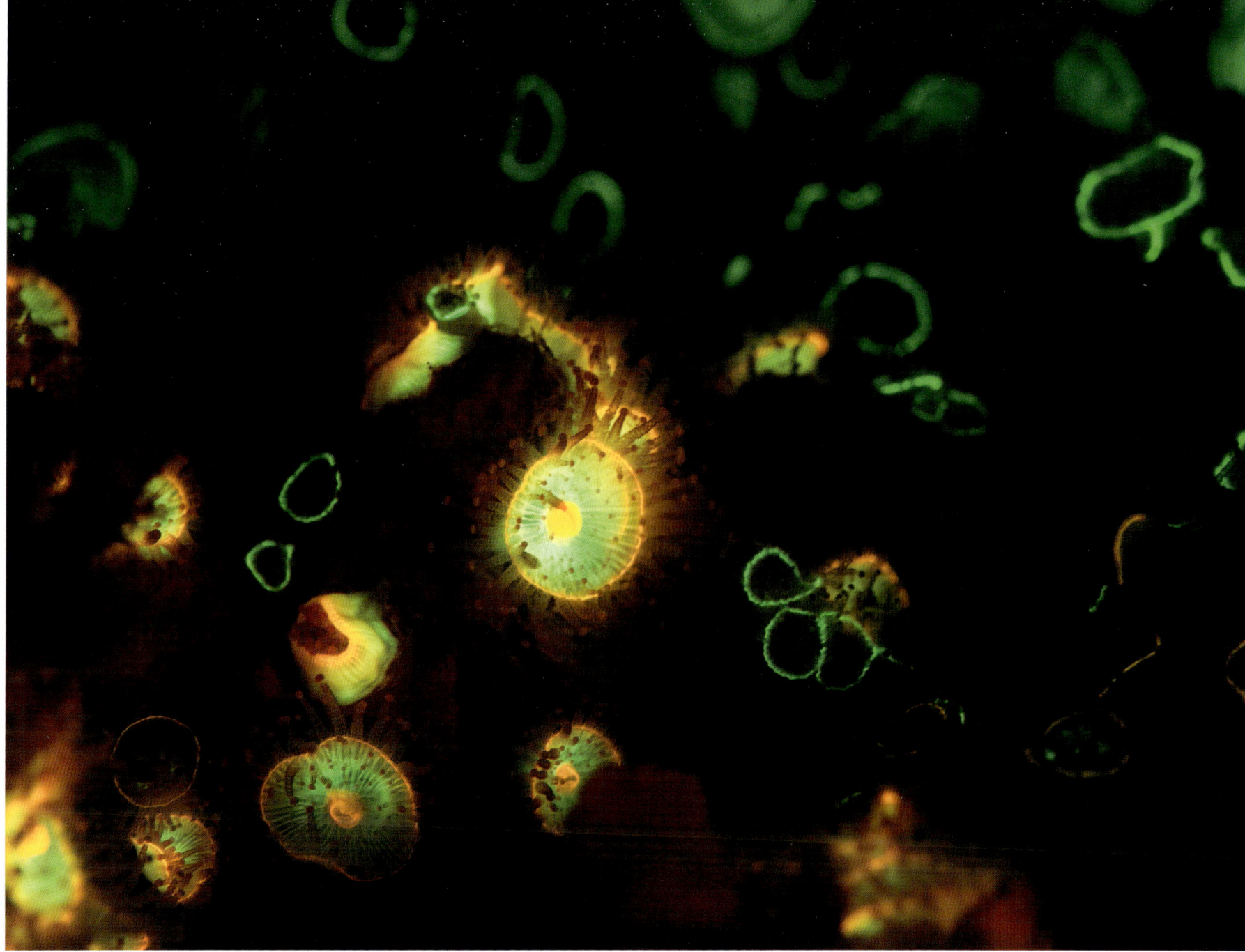

Underwater Garden
Botanical Britain | Highly Commended

Jacob Guy
Jewel anemone (*Corynactis viridis*)
Torquay, Dorset, England

Panasonic GH5 Mark II with Olympus 60mm f/2.8 Macro lens. 60mm; 1/80th second; f/5.6; ISO 640.

When people think of colour under the water, they usually think of tropical coral reefs. However, our British waters are home to an abundance of colour, including these jewel anemones. Even though they are colourful during the day, at night and under fluorescent lighting even more colours are revealed in this miniature underwater meadow.

Ghost
Animal Portraits

Rosalie Smith
Barn owl (*Tyto alba*)
Kent, England

Canon R5 with Canon EF 500mm f/4L II lens. 500mm; 1/2,000th second; f/4; ISO 400.

It was a stunning winter evening, just before dusk, when an unforgettable moment unfolded. I could hardly believe my luck as I spotted an owl flying by and managed to capture a few shots just as it silently landed. After the barn owl touched down on a nearby post, it took off again and caught a large vole. It's moments like these that make wildlife photography truly magical.

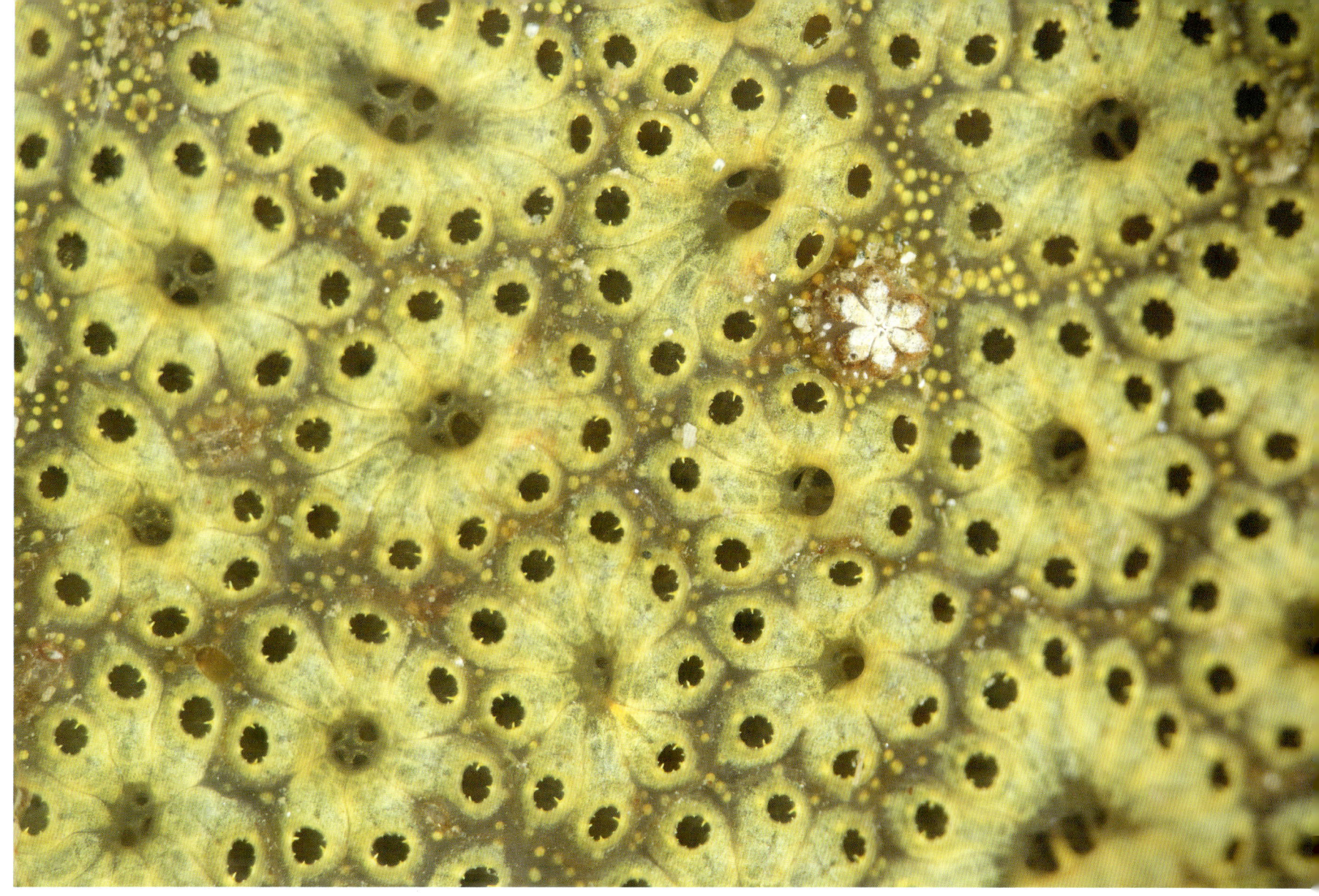

Never Alone
Hidden Britain

Sandra Stalker
Star ascidian (*Botryllus schlosseri*)
Porthkerris, Cornwall, England

Sony A7R IV with Sony FE 90mm f/2.8 G Macro lens. 90mm; 1/100th second; f/11; ISO 250.

A small colony of white-coloured star ascidian sea squirts is growing on top of a pale yellow-green colony at Porthkerris. Star ascidians are purported to be one of the closest living invertebrates to humans. These sea squirts are amazing in their ability to regenerate damaged tissue from their vascular system alone and it is thought that they may contribute to scientific studies on the human vascular system and even potentially the regeneration of limbs. Not only are they a beautiful natural form but they also demonstrate the interconnectedness of our species.

Coastal Wild Flowers
Botanical Britain

Sarah Williams
Viper's bugloss, Evening primrose and Bunnytail grass
Minehead, Somerset, England

Canon 7D Mark II with Canon EF 18-200mm f/3.5-5.6 lens. 32mm; 1/30th second; f/11; ISO 100.

I took this photo during the golden hour along the England Coast Path between Minehead and Dunster in June. The low sun was illuminating the bank of wildflowers consisting of viper's bugloss, bunnytail grass and evening primrose.

Painted Wood
Botanical Britain

Ian Wade
Bluebells (*Hyacinthoides non-scripta*)
Somerset, England

Canon 5D Mark II with Canon EF 100-400mm f/4.5-5.6L lens. 190mm; 1/125th second; f/5; ISO 400.

Trying to capture a very popular subject differently is always a challenge. I decided to photograph bluebells in my local wood using a technique that would make the flowers look like a painting. By getting down low, pushing my lens into the bluebells and focusing on one subject, I was able to blur the rest and create a cool-looking image.

Coastal Contrasts

Botanical Britain | Highly Commended

Francesca Page

Japanese wireweed (*Sargassum muticum*)
Man o' War Cove, Dorset, England

Sony A7 IV with Sony FE 12-24mm f/4 G lens. 12mm; 1/200th second; f/18; ISO 160.

On Dorset's Jurassic Coast, this split shot contrasts serene cliffs with invasive Japanese Wireweed below. Capturing this image took months of planning for perfect alignment between cliff and wireweed, under ideal conditions of clear water, no wind, and low tide. Using a 12mm wide-angle lens at f/18 and an underwater strobe, I highlighted the yellow hues of the wireweed against the blue water and green cliffs. Rapidly spreading since 1973, wireweed disrupts native species but also offers habitats for marine life. This photo captures environmental struggles often hidden in plain sight, even at major UK tourist spots.

Rainbow Sea Slug in the Kelp
Coast & Marine | Highly Commended

Martin Stevens
Rainbow sea slug (*Babakina anadoni*)
Falmouth, Cornwall, England

Olympus EM5 Mark III with Olympus 60mm f/2.8 Macro lens. 60mm; 1/250th second; f/9; ISO 250.

The rainbow sea slug is a new arrival to UK waters, first discovered only a few years ago on the Isles of Scilly. I was fortunate enough to find some of the first individuals from the mainland on the Cornish coast. This sea slug was found among the kelp exposed on a low spring tide. The photo is an in-camera double exposure, combining a macro photo of the tiny slug on the kelp, taken with a snoot, and a wide-angle split shot of the habitat at the same location not long after with a fisheye lens.

The Knockout Blow
Animal Behaviour

Mark Cooper
Brown hare (*Lepus europaeus*)
Woodford Valley, Salisbury, Wiltshire, England

Sony a1 with Sony FE 600mm f/4 GM lens. 600mm; 1/1,000th second; f/4; ISO 1,600.

An August morning in the Woodford Valley in the Wiltshire countryside, near my hometown of Salisbury, and I was looking to photograph red kites. But then I noticed a couple of brown hares in the field behind me. Quickly, I repositioned myself, resting my camera and lens on a gatepost. I stayed perfectly still, and to my surprise and delight this pair started to box in perfect light. Out of 180 shots in six seconds of intense action, I decided this was probably the decisive blow!

Buzzard Standoff
Animal Behaviour

Mike Tibbotts
Common buzzard (*Buteo buteo*)
Surrey, England

Nikon Z 8 with Nikon Z 800mm f/6.3 lens. 800mm; 1/500th second; f/6.3; ISO 9,000.

A pair of buzzards fighting over territorial rights. This is typical behaviour, with a display of outstretched wings and aggressive posturing. The pair were arguing over a hare carcass (roadkill) that I positioned safely away from the highway to see what might turn up to feed on it. There were also other scavengers at the scene, including magpies and crows, so the action was pretty intense at some points, with the buzzards exerting their superiority over them as well as each other.

Black Guillemot
Animal Portraits

Chris Hawes
Black guillemot (*Cepphus grylle*)
Oban, Argyll and Bute, Scotland

Canon 7D Mark II with Canon EF 300mm f/2.8L II lens and 2x teleconverter. 600mm; 1/1,600th second; f/5.6; ISO 800.

I enjoy photographing wildfowl from a surface-level position and have often photographed various ducks, grebes, divers etc., this way. On a visit to the west coast of Scotland, I spotted a group of black guillemots on the water and decided to attempt the same thing. After a careful approach over slippery rocks and seaweed, I was able to get into position at the water's edge, and it was then a case of waiting for one of them to come close enough for an image. The bright background colour is from a boat moored a short distance away.

Pas de Deux ▶
Animal Portraits

Diana Schmies
Black guillemot (*Cepphus grylle*)
Oban, Argyll and Bute, Scotland

Nikon D500 with Tamron 70-200mm f/2.8 lens. 200mm; 1/640th second; f/2.8; ISO 800.

During my two-day stay in Oban, I had the privilege of photographing the captivating mating dance of black guillemots. The birds were chasing and stalking each other back and forth, running in circles, either strutting with a high-stepped walk or crouching, with upstretched necks and down-pointed bills, mostly in pairs and sometimes in groups, all while being very vocal. As I had to deal with very poor light and a less appealing backdrop, I chose to create high-key images that solely emphasised the black guillemots' distinctive features and their characteristic postures during the display.

Nuts about Nuts!
Animal Portraits

Jed Lawson
Red squirrel (*Sciurus vulgaris*)
Aberdeenshire, Scotland

Sony A7R III with Sony FE 200-600mm f/5.6-6.3 G lens. 600mm; 1/2,000th second; f/8; ISO 4,000.

This photo was taken at a hide local to me in Aberdeenshire. This red squirrel was the highlight of my day watching these funny yet intriguing characters! This red in particular knew how to pose for me! Using the lovely gnarled wood as a perch, the perfectly matching purple heather in front contrasted with the bright colours of this red. A bait of hazelnuts and other nuts was used.

Weasel at Rush Hour

Urban Wildlife | Highly Commended

Tom Kelly

Weasel (*Mustela nivalis*)
Edinburgh, Scotland

Nikon Z 9 with Nikon Z 180-600mm f/5.6-6.3 lens. 340mm; 1/400th second; f/6.3; ISO 4,000.

There simply wasn't time to plan this shot as a weasel popped its head up and then dashed across a road into the vegetation. Photographing a weasel in the centre of Edinburgh would have been good enough for me, but my mind seemed to shout 'urban shot' at me. With my lens wide open and fully extended to 600mm focal length, I quickly gave it one turn and adjusted it to just under 400mm. This enabled me to capture the road sign behind it and the double red lines in front of it – they're fast wee guys!

Ptarmigan
Animal Portraits

Chris Hawes
Ptarmigan (*Lagopus muta*)
Cairngorms, Scotland

Canon 1D X Mark II with Canon EF 300mm f/2.8L II lens and 2x teleconverter. 600mm; 1/3,200th second; f/8; ISO 800.

I enjoy spending time up in the Scottish mountains, but I face a dilemma every single time over whether to pack my camera. The additional weight makes a huge difference on long hikes or in tough conditions and, invariably, when I do carry it I fail to find any wildlife. Conversely, on the days I leave it behind, I seem to have lovely close encounters with various mountain species. On this day, however, my luck changed, and I had my camera in hand as this male ptarmigan stepped out from the rocks into the last moments of sunlight hitting the ridge.

The Call of the Wild
Animal Behaviour

Heshan Peiris
Red deer (*Cervus elaphus*)
Richmond Park, London, England

Nikon D850 with Nikon 400mm f/2.8 lens.
400mm; 1/1,250th second; f/2,8; ISO 560.

One of my dreams was to capture a red deer in a misty atmosphere. Though it had been gloomy for weeks, with relentless scattering showers, I packed my camera gear and cycled towards Richmond Park to make my wish come true. Being Asian, it's tough to bear the freezing weather, but my ambitious self made me roam around the park for an hour to find a herd of stags. It was the rutting season and I had heard that the male stags become very aggressive. I was stunned to find a large stag bellowing out in the shadows, and making my day luckier, a ray of golden sun touched the park. I became determined to capture a stag in this golden, stunning atmosphere. My luck and patience paid off as the large stag came out of the shadows and bellowed out right in front of me for a few seconds before chasing a female stag. It was one of the best moments of my wildlife journey. All of a sudden, the weather changed and the golden atmosphere disappeared within half an hour. I was so happy about the outcome I achieved under the challenging weather and the tight time frame.

Hare in Motion
Animal Portraits | Winner

David Tipling
Brown hare (*Lepus europaeus*)
Norfolk, England

OM System OM-1 with OM 150-600mm f/5-6.3 lens. 400mm; 1/10th second; f/6.1; ISO 200.

The late artist Robert Gillmor created a beautiful linocut of a running hare, showing the different positions a hare's legs take as they run. I thought it would be interesting to try to recreate this piece of art in a photograph by using a slow shutter speed of 1/10 sec as a hare ran. It took many attempts, photographing hares as they ran up and down a field of winter wheat, but I finally achieved this image of a hare in motion.

The Roost
Coast & Marine

David Tipling
Oystercatcher (*Haematopus ostralegus*)
Snettisham, Norfolk, England

Olympus E-M1X with Olympus 150-400mm f/4.5 lens. 288mm; 1/10th second; f/13; ISO 64.

These oystercatchers were flying to roost at Snettisham on The Wash. Many small flocks flew past, giving me repeated opportunities to experiment with motion blur. I used a slow shutter speed of 1/10 sec while panning as the birds flew by to create this image, which I felt was the most interesting from the images I captured that afternoon.

Toad in the Road
Animal Behaviour

Peter Brooks
Common toad (*Bufo bufo*)
Sussex, England

Nikon D500 with Nikon 24-70mm f/2.8 lens. 24mm; 1/160th second; f/4; ISO 200.

Photographing the toads crossing the road, I wanted to capture how dangerous this was for them and the dangers they face. After finding several dead toads and witnessing many close calls, I moved my own van into the background of my shot with the headlights backlighting the toad. Lying in the road, I used a wide-angle lens to capture the full scene and an off-camera flash on low power to front light the toad without overpowering the beautiful light bouncing off the rain-soaked road. It was this moment of peril and beauty that I wanted to convey.

Toadally Being Watched
Animal Portraits

Andrew Wood
Common toad (*Bufo bufo*)
Bourne Woods, Lincolnshire, England

Sony A7S III with Sony FE 100-400mm f/4.5-5.6 GM lens. 400mm; 1/500th second; f/5.6; ISO 800.

Out walking, I found a pond and flooded puddles full of toads. I went to get my camera and tried to bring some ideas to life. This reflection shot is an image I have wanted to capture for a long time. It took a while to find the right toad, puddle and background. This toad was particularly obliging and allowed me to take multiple shots from different angles. I revisited a few days later and they had almost all returned to the forest, reinforcing my belief that wildlife photography is often about being in the right place at the right time.

Butterfly Face-off
Animal Behaviour | Winner

John Waters
Speckled wood (*Pararge aegeria*)
Bristol, England

Canon 5D Mark III with Laowa 24mm f/14 Probe lens. 24mm; 1/4th second; ISO 320.

In a small block of deciduous woodland on the outskirts of Bristol, I wanted to photograph the aerial chases of the speckled wood butterfly. In spring, males stake out a sunny patch along a woodland path and will chase off any rival male that comes too close, usually spiralling up into the canopy. On this occasion, a prolonged chase occurred about 1.5m above the ground and I could approach quite close to get several shots. I was extremely lucky with this image in that it shows the instant that one of the butterflies has spun around to face its pursuer.

Crab Rider
Coast & Marine | Highly Commended

Kirsty Andrews
Crab and Medusa (*Arthropoda* and *Hydromedusa*)
Loch Carron, Scotland

Nikon D500 with Nikon 60mm f/2.8 lens. 60mm; 1/250th second; f/20; ISO 250.

Travelling the oceans at any time are innumerable larval animals running the gauntlet of predators and food sources, perhaps hoping to settle on the seabed, if they make it that far. A tiny crustacean, such as this crab, may use a jellyfish or hydromedusa for camouflage and propulsion, helping it navigate the vast sea. Photos like this are more commonly seen in exotic landscapes, but they are present in UK waters as well and a treat to see if you look carefully for tiny subjects drifting through the water.

Caledonian Corona
Wild Woods

Graham Niven
Caledonian pine (*Pinus sylvestris*)
Cairngorms, Scotland

Nikon D850 with Nikon 20mm f/1.8 lens. 20mm; 6 seconds; f/1.8; ISO 400.

10th May 2024 – a night that will live long in the memory. The aurora borealis forecast was for a strong showing, but my initial plans to capture it were scuppered by cloud cover. As the sky finally cleared, it was late and I headed to a nearby location in the Caledonian pine forest of Abernethy in the Cairngorms where I would ordinarily go for a good view north. When I arrived, I realised that it was bursting with activity all over the sky. This shot is looking directly up into the eye of an aurora 'corona', or 'crown', where the rays appear to converge, framed by the surrounding trees. As it pulsed and danced, I thought I was going to be beamed into space. I was standing in almost complete silence, except for the clicking of bats skimming the water nearby, and at one point the silhouette of an owl flew silently through. A magical experience.

Forked Birch
Wild Woods | Runner-up

Tim George
Holme Fen,
Cambridgeshire, England

Fujifilm GFX 100 with Fujifilm 20-35mm f/4 lens. 35mm; 480 seconds; f/8; ISO 100.

This image was taken in ancient fen woodland, an hour after nightfall. It was set up in the last of the daylight and taken when it had become completely dark to the naked eye. The eight-minute exposure brought out the light in the sky. This was balanced with one battery-operated portable tube light placed on either side of the tree and set, after experimentation, to 5500 Kelvin colour temperature and 2% light output. It was taken in winter using such subdued lighting in order to cause minimum disruption to flora and fauna.

Autumn Birches
Wild Woods

James Roddie
Silver birch (*Betula pendula*)
Glen Affric, Scotland

Nikon Z 9 with Nikon Z 24-120mm f/4 lens. 75mm; 0.4 seconds; f/11; ISO 100.

Several days of misty mornings in Glen Affric produced some beautiful conditions for photography. One morning was frustrating, as each time I reached my intended location the mist would disperse with remarkable speed. I got to this particular spot just in time, however. As the mist started to shift, it revealed these elegant silver birches adorned with vivid colours.

A Living Flame
Botanical Britain

Dan Bolt
Flame shell and Cartilaginous cock's comb
(*Limaria hians* and *Plocamium cartilagineum*)
Loch Carron, Scotland

OM System OM-1 with Olympus 12-50mm f/3.5-6.3 lens. 50mm; 1/100th second; f/8; ISO 200.

Diving in a protected marine habitat is always an honour, and as one of Scotland's largest known flame shell beds, diving on this site in Loch Carron is truly a magical experience. This rare mollusc is usually concealed below a thick matting of marine life, but occasionally one can be seen out in the open. I was immediately taken by the flame-like colours, textures and forms of both the flame shell and the branching fronds of the scarlet seaweed immediately in front of it.

Breaking Down
Botanical Britain

Andrew Neal
Walnut tree (*Juglans sp.*)
Back Garden, Essex, England

Olympus E-M1 Mark II with Olympus 90mm f/3.5 lens. 90mm; 1/50th second; f/6.3; ISO 200.

In order to bring out as much detail as possible when photographing this walnut leaf, I used a combination of backlighting and diffused on-camera flash. Looking at the whole leaf, I experimented with ways of framing the shot to find the most interesting section to capture. Some areas of the leaf were completely brown, while others were still green and healthy. By diagonally framing the stark transition between the two, I wanted the viewer to almost feel as if they could see the leaf breaking down in front of their eyes.

Orchid Dawn
Botanical Britain

Simon Carder
Green-winged orchids (*Anacamptis morio*)
Chew Valley Lake, Somerset, England

Canon R5 with Sigma 180mm f/2.8 Macro lens. 180mm; 1/2,500th second; f/2.8; ISO 100.

This is a 10-image, in-camera focus stack of green-winged orchids. It was taken after dawn one morning, lying down and handheld, using my elbows and body as a natural tripod to keep the camera steady. I shot through other orchids and wildflowers to add additional colour to the image. I always take a yoga mat with me when photographing orchids and wear full waterproofs (it's always wet at dawn in April and May). This is partly to stay reasonably dry, but I also lay the mat on the ground to ensure I have enough space without crushing any of the surrounding orchids. If the mat doesn't fit, I move on or find a different composition.

Black Grouse
Animal Portraits

Ian Mason
Black grouse
(*Lyrurus tetrix*)
Perthshire, Scotland

Canon 1D X with Canon EF 600mm f/4L lens. 600mm; 1/500th second; f/4; ISO 1,600.

On a bleak, exposed Perthshire mountain in mid-winter, I helped a friend build a small private hide, where he had watched a very small lek over several years. A few weeks later, it blew down and was retrieved 100 metres away and rebuilt! Only a few birds appeared, but that meant I could concentrate on one or two without distraction. The sun rising over the hills behind produced some beautiful light on the subject and background hills.

Rest in Peace
Animal Portraits

Roy McDonald
Mute swan (*Cygnus olor*)
Tring, England

Nikon D500 with Nikon 500mm f/5.6 lens. 500mm; 1/1,000th second; f/5.6, ISO 100.

This image holds a very powerful emotion for me. I had just received very sad news of the passing of my father's sister after a long battle with dementia and decided to turn to nature, as I always do, to cope. Whilst sitting in contemplation, this majestic swan swam towards me in the early morning mist – a beautiful symbol of peace and a welcomeness of calm, with a happy reminder of a soul now at peace.

Chirping to the Moon
Black & White

Matt Stuttard Parker
Robin (*Erithacus rubecula*)
Wareham, Dorset, England

Sony A7 IV with Sigma 100-400mm f/5-6.3 Contemporary lens. 370mm; 1/400th second; f/6.3; ISO 500.

After shooting the full moon over a local landmark, I came home to this robin in a nearby tree happily chirping away and managed not to scare it away whilst getting out of the car! I've always wanted to photograph a bird silhouetted by a full moon and was lucky it sat singing for long enough for me to capture! I love the high contrast the moon provides in black and white silhouettes and was super pleased to finally get this shot.

Puffin
Animal Portraits

Chris Hawes
Atlantic puffin (*Fratercula arctica*)
Skomer Island, Pembrokeshire, Wales

Canon 1D X Mark II with Canon EF 300mm f/2.8L II lens and 1.4x teleconverter. 420mm; 1/2,500th second; f/4; ISO 800.

During a fantastic stay on Skomer Island, I was treated to a couple of stunning sunrises and the early alarm clock was rewarded with some images of the puffins in the beautiful light. On this occasion, I was able to capture some silhouette images of a bird as it positioned itself directly in front of the low sun.

Red Grouse Coming in to Land
Animal Portraits | Runner-up

Ben Hall
Red grouse (*Lagopus lagopus*)
Yorkshire Dales National Park, England

Canon 1D X Mark II with Canon EF 500mm f/4L lens. 500mm; 1/640th second; f/5.6; ISO 2,000.

I spent several days photographing the red grouse that frequent the Yorkshire moors. I had positioned myself not far from a male grouse that was feeding on heather. While taking images of the grouse feeding, I noticed a second bird flying in. I had just enough time to reposition myself and capture the moment it came in to land on the heather with wings outstretched.

Ptarmigan Viewpoint
Habitat

Jamie McDermaid
Ptarmigan (*Lagopus muta*)
Loch Lomond, Scotland

Nikon D810 with Nikon 35mm f/1.8 lens. 35mm; 1/640th second; f/8; ISO 360.

This image of a ptarmigan looking out over Scotland's Southern Highlands was a chance encounter on an early spring hike up Beinn Narnain. Having found myself previously lagging behind my friends with my large lens in tow, I resorted to bringing the lighter 35mm lens this time in the hope that I'd still be able to capture some wildlife-in-landscape images. I expected to encounter a few ravens, but this ptarmigan was a very nice surprise as it posed on a lovely vantage point overlooking its vast and rugged home.

Eye to Eye
Animal Portraits | Highly Commended

Philip Male
Kestrel (*Falco tinnunculus*)
Broad Town, Wiltshire, England

Canon R3 with Canon EF 600mm f/4L II lens and 1.4x teleconverter. 840mm; 1/4,000th second; f/5.6; ISO 3,200.

At 840mm, this female kestrel was farther away than she looks, but to be honest I was waiting for the thud on the front of the lens! She was skimming over the grass heads to who knows where, but she gave me a good look before she veered off. This image was taken in the field behind my house in Wiltshire.

Stone Walled
Urban Wildlife

Ian Wood
Badger (*Meles meles*)
Chilfrome, Dorset, England

Nikon Z 9 with Nikon 70-200mm f/2.8G lens. 116mm; 1/40th second; f/3.5; ISO 10,000.

A friend painted this fox onto my garden wall and I spent an insane amount of time waiting in a hide to see if any animals passed by. The only lighting is the four weak solar downlights, so I had to push the ISO quite high for this shot. After several months, my favourite shot was this badger, which briefly paused near the fox artwork.

Line Dancing
Urban Wildlife

Paul Goldstein
Red fox (*Vulpes vulpes*)
Wimbledon, England

Canon 1D X Mark III with Canon EF 70-200mm f/2.8L II lens. 160mm; 1/400th second; f/2.8; ISO 400.

Urban foxes are now incredibly common and excellent photographic subjects, however, this was unusual. I had seen a small family a few times as I crossed this tramline on my daily run, so one evening I tucked myself down by the line. They were foraging along the track but were not very bothered by me, or indeed any other commuters. Whether it was a scent or just inquisitiveness I don't know, but this young one then walked down the line towards me. Perhaps they find it easier on the smooth track than on the rougher sleepers; I don't know, but they seemed to know when to scarper when the trams travelled by.

Slow Journey Under Darkness
Urban Wildlife | Highly Commended

Ian Wade
Garden snail (*Cornu aspersum*)
Bristol, England

Canon 5D Mark III with Venus Optics 15mm Macro lens. 15mm; 0.4 seconds; ISO 1,000.

One evening, I spotted this snail on a scaffolding pole on our house. I quickly grabbed my camera with its wide-angle macro lens and used my mobile phone as a light source. It was tricky balancing a longer exposure to bring out the environmental details while keeping the snail in shape. After a few failed images, I captured this one.

Splashing Around
Habitat

Phil James
Grey seal (*Halichoerus grypus*)
Norfolk, England

Canon 1D X Mark II with Canon EF 600mm f/4L II lens. 600mm; 1/800th second; f/5.6; ISO 200.

I headed to the north Norfolk coast on a sunny but cold afternoon in January. Using one of the groynes as a hide, I patiently waited for some seals to come past. This female grey seal returned to the beach and started to haul out. She paused briefly in the surf, with the incoming waves breaking over her back and spraying foam everywhere. This made for good natural framing and added some drama to the image. She then continued up the beach to relax with the rest of the colony.

Embraced by Waves
Black & White

Diana Schmies
Grey seal (*Halichoerus grypus*)
Llandudno Bay, Wales

Nikon D500 with Tamron 70-200mm f/2.8 lens. 92mm; 1/500th second; f/7.1; ISO 1,600.

Seals, as semi-aquatic mammals, have the intriguing habit of splitting their time between the coasts and the oceans, following the rhythm of the tides. After resting on a small beach in North Wales, this female seal was the first to return to the open sea as soon as the water started to rise. The foamy wave encircled her body as if the ocean was welcoming her back with a soft hug. When the scene unfolded, I perceived everything in slow motion. Nevertheless, I triggered the burst mode to ensure that I did not miss this magical yet fleeting moment.

Power Dive
Animal Portraits

David Pressland
Northern gannet (*Morus bassanus*)
Staithes, North Yorkshire, England

Nikon D850 with Nikon 300mm f/4 lens.
300mm; 1/2,500th second; f/5.6; ISO 200.

A third-year juvenile gannet goes into a power dive. These birds can reach speeds of 60mph when they hit the water and they have built-in shock absorbers to prevent damage from the impact. This image was taken on a whale and dolphin-watching trip out of Staithes, North Yorkshire.

Eat, Sleep, Play, Repeat
Animal Portraits | Highly Commended

Alison Vaughan
Otter (*Lutra lutra*)
Isle of Mull, Scotland

Nikon D500 with Nikon 200-500mm f/5.6 lens. 210mm; 1/320th second; f/5.6; ISO 200.

The Isle of Mull: a lifetime dream to see otters. Lying quietly behind a large rock in the wet kelp, I had the privilege to share the intimacy of these two cubs catching a variety of fish to eat, playing together in the water and then crashing out, exhausted by their antics. They slept soundly for half an hour and slipped back into the water with their mother to continue their journey. What a real honour, and definitely a heart-thumping moment.

The Peak District in Infrared
Black & White

Justin Minns
The Peak District, England

Canon R5 with Canon RF 24-105mm f/4L lens. 58mm; 2.5 seconds; f/8; ISO 1,600.

This was one of those days when the shadows from drifting cumulus clouds scudded over the dramatic ridges of Chrome and Parkhouse Hills in the Peak District. I used an infrared filter to highlight this effect, and as the light and shadow moved over the landscape, I waited until the sun came out on this group of trees before pressing the shutter.

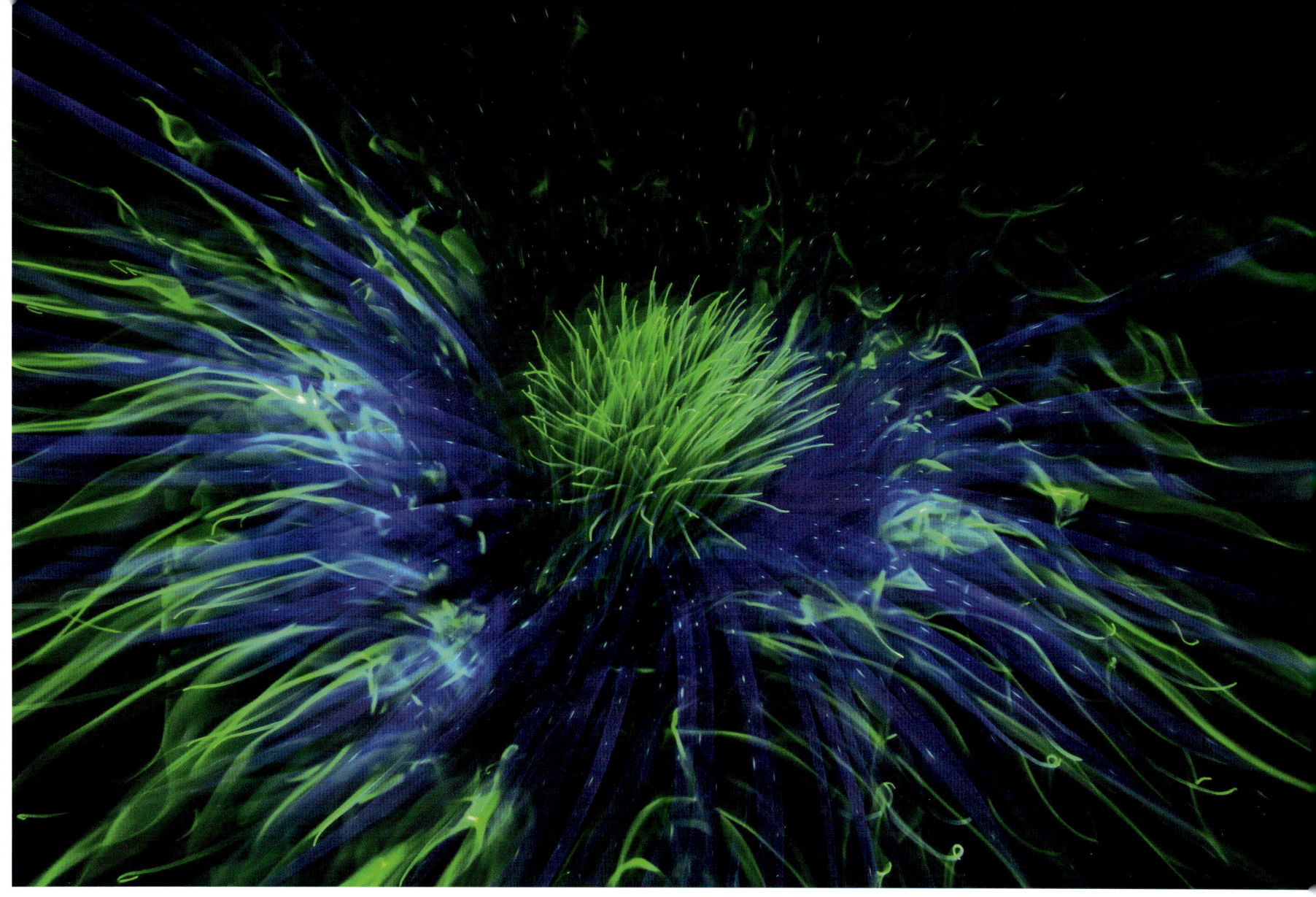

Fluorescent Fire
Coast & Marine | Highly Commended

James Lynott
Fireworks anemone (*Pachycerianthus multiplicatus*)
Inveraray, Loch Fyne, Scotland

Canon G7X Mark III. 9mm; 0.8 seconds; f/9; ISO 125.

I have seen many incredible examples of slow-shutter images from other photographers, but I had never seen this technique combined with underwater fluorescence, so this was something I was keen to try. I experimented with a range of subjects and discovered I really liked how fireworks anemones looked using this technique, which was not really a surprise, as they are my favourite fluoro subject! This shot was captured during a pre-sunrise dive in Loch Fyne in October.

Storm Warning
Black & White

Brian Matthews
Between Mull and Tiree, Scotland

Canon 1D X with Canon EF 70-200mm f/2.8L II lens. 70mm; 1/320th second; f/5.6; ISO 200.

On a calm summer day in the Inner Hebrides, I sailed out in search of basking sharks, but within an hour the sky darkened ominously. A tropical storm off Scotland was brewing! This is an image of a storm, but it's a story about climate change.

The UK had been experiencing a record-breaking heatwave, with temperatures exceeding 40°C, and a severe thunderstorm was forming as hot air from the Scottish coast clashed with cold Atlantic air. I captured the brooding sky and the approaching downpour before racing to shelter on the Isle of Coll. This rare Hebridean storm, intensified by climate change, is a stark reminder of the increasing frequency of extreme weather events.

Red Deer Stag Shaking Off Rain
Animal Behaviour | Highly Commended

Neil McIntyre
Red deer (*Cervus elaphus*)
Western Highlands, Scotland

Nikon Z 9 with Nikon 500mm f/5.6 PF lens. 500mm; 1/500th second; f/5.6; ISO 1,250.

A horrible wet day is not normally the type you would choose to go out photographing in; however, if you do make the effort, you can sometimes be rewarded with more unique results. This shaking-off-rain image is a perfect example. If the deer is lying down and rain has soaked into its coat, there is a fair chance that when it stands up it will shake. Camera at the ready, you sometimes have to wait a fair while for the animal to stand, but on this occasion it was no longer than a few minutes. In fact, I just got the camera on him in time to capture the moment, knowing its head always stays perfectly still throughout the shake. I usually select a slowish shutter speed to show a bit of movement in the coat.

Mandarin Love
Habitat

Andrew Rouse
Mandarin duck (*Aix galericulata*)
England

OM System OM-1 with OM 150-400mm f/4.5 TC lens. 500mm; 1/1,250th second; f/5.6; ISO 1,600.

I'm lucky enough to have a Mandarin duck roost close enough to me to head there when the weather looks interesting. By interesting, I mean cold and misty. In these conditions, I always approach them to shoot backlit, as I want to capture something worthwhile, not a record shot. They are exceptionally shy, so I keep my distance and arrive well before dawn.

There are a few places that I know well where the sun breaks through the trees; on this morning, right in that spot, a male and female were quietly sleeping. I just love the peace and tranquillity of this shot. All ducks are beautiful to me, but the mandarins present an added challenge.

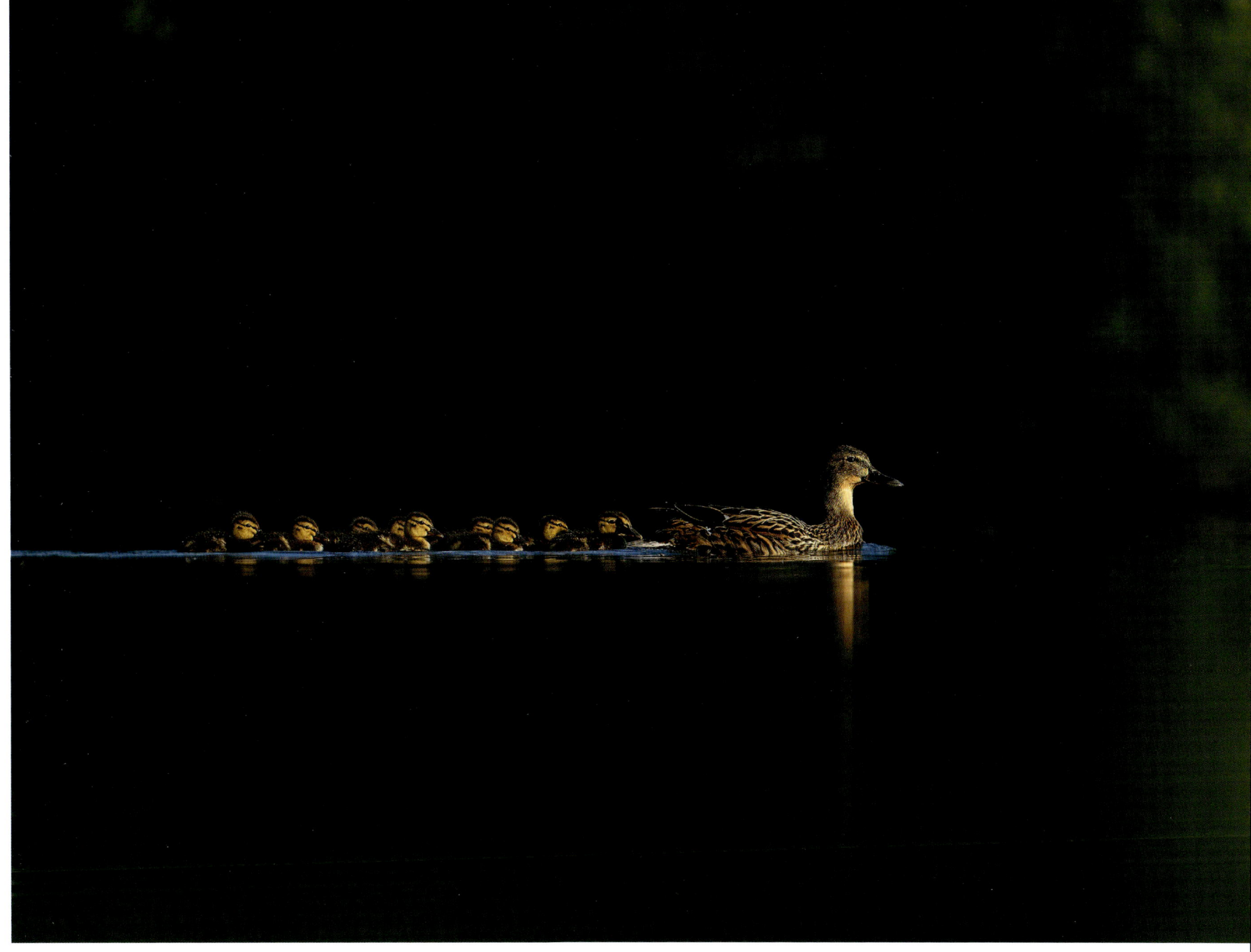

School Run
Animal Behaviour

Ben Marsh
Mallard (*Anas platyrhynchos*)
Derbyshire, England

Sony A7 II with Sony FE 200-600mm f/5.6-6.3 G lens. 388mm; 1/1,250th second; f/6.3; ISO 200.

I took this photo in the early hours of a summer morning in Derbyshire. A fellow photographer and I carried our cameras and tripods down a steep bank and set up to wait on the edge of a lake, sitting in a couple of inches of water with our lenses level to the surface. We were there to photograph a pair of swans that were raising cygnets of their own, but instead we had our attention stolen by this mother duck and her ducklings.

Quartering
Animal Behaviour

Helen Jackson-Garside
Short-eared owl (*Asio flammeus*)
Hawling, Gloucestershire, England

Canon 1D X Mark II with Canon EF 600mm f/4L III lens and 1.4x teleconverter. 840mm; 1/2,000th second; f/5.6; ISO 1,600.

A beautiful short-eared owl locked eyes with me briefly as it banked round a turn while hunting for voles over rough grassland. Their visits are fleeting, but every moment spent in their company is treasured. Photographed from behind a stone wall next to a footpath, patience was rewarded for hours spent freezing atop a windy hill. The cold is immediately forgotten once the owls are in the air!

Mouse Battle
Animal Behaviour | Highly Commended

Terry Whittaker
House mouse (*Mus musculus*)
Manchester, England

Nikon D600 (Infrared Converted) with Nikon 85mm f/1.8 lens. 85mm; 1/200th second; f/16; ISO 400.

I discovered that the small population of house mice that live under my garden shed had managed to get into it by gnawing a hole through the planking. This gave them access to my store of bird food. I put most of the bird food into a metal container to prevent this but made some available to them in paper bags in order to photograph them. I used an infra-red converted DSLR camera trap with a motion sensor and three infra-red filtered flashes, one of which was on a higher output than the others and fired through a sheet of cardboard with slits cut in it to give the shadow effect. With the camera in a relatively soundproof box and the mice unable to see the flash, I was able to capture a range of natural behaviours.

Storm Light Over the Caledonian Forest
Wild Woods | Winner

James Roddie
Scots pine (*Pinus sylvestris*)
Glen Strathfarrar, Scotland

Nikon Z 7 with Nikon Z 24-70mm f/4 lens.
28mm; 1/160th second; f/9; ISO 160.

Stormy days in the Scottish Highlands can produce some wonderful light for photography. I headed out with my camera to a location I had never visited before and could immediately see the photographic potential of these old Scots pine trees. I waited in heavy rain for quite a while, and my luck came when a burst of light illuminated the trees perfectly with a rainbow behind.

Clinging On to Life
Botanical Britain

Christopher Rutter
Hawthorn bush
(*Crataegus monogyna*)
Glen Suardale, Isle of Skye,
Scotland

Nikon Z 7 with Nikon 17-35mm f/2.8 lens. 19mm; 2.5 seconds; f/22; ISO 100.

I found a small number of stunted hawthorn bushes growing in a gryke in a small patch of limestone pavement above Glen Suardale that perfectly illustrates the struggle for survival in this harsh location. I chose this one as the main foreground, beaten down by the wind and weather, as it was the most photogenic. I then had to wait for an hour or so for rain and sleet showers to pass over the distant peak of Beinn na Caillich to capture this image of both the hawthorn and the weather that it has to endure.

Dipper Falls
Habitat

Charles Everitt
White-throated dipper (*Cinclus cinclus*)
River Esk, Dalkeith, Scotland

Canon 5D Mark IV with Canon EF 500mm f/4L lens.
500mm; 1/6th second; f/16; ISO 100.

Having discovered the dipper's nest beside the falls the previous year, I returned the following spring with this image in mind. I watched the bird's behaviour to determine the optimum moment to press the cable release to soften the waterfall while keeping the bird sharp. The dippers never stayed on the stone for long, but they usually landed around the same spot, allowing me to pre-focus and lock up the camera's mirror as a bird flew in. The image places the dipper firmly in its river habitat, on which it relies for sourcing food, nesting sites and breeding.

Rim-lit Siskin
Animal Portraits

Stephen Street
Siskin (*Spinus spinus*)
North Yorkshire, England

Canon R3 with Canon EF 500mm f/4L lens and 1.4x teleconverter. 700mm; 1/640th second; f/7.1; ISO 8,000.

There are rows of trees along the edge of my garden that seem to be a highway for visiting birds. Among them was a hawthorn that seemed to be particularly popular. I noticed that in the late afternoon backlighting would break through for a couple of hours. When the light looked promising, I would set up my camera and tripod and wait to see what happened. The lighting conditions only lasted for about a week before creeping shadows snuffed them out. During my third session, this male siskin landed fleetingly at the ideal angle for capturing the rim-lighting effect.

◀ **Fierce Fight**
Animal Behaviour

Harry King
Red fox (*Vulpes vulpes*)
Bristol, England

Canon 7D Mark II with Sigma 10-20mm f/4-5.6 lens. 17mm; 1/125th second; f/4.5; ISO 100.

This image captures foxes fighting over territories, showing how ferocious they can be while protecting themselves and trying to keep others away from their territory. I took this image using a zoom lens and flash to keep my distance from the foxes so they would show their natural behaviour. From the start of the mating season through September to November, the foxes will do anything to keep others from taking their habitat and will fight very viciously to protect their families. Sometimes, while fighting, they will make extremely loud screaming sounds that sound like a baby crying.

Ruthless Rumble
Animal Behaviour

Syed Muhammad Irtiza Usman
Coot (*Fulica atra*)
Cardiff, Wales

Sony A6700 with Sony FE 200-600mm f/5.6-6.3 G lens. 600mm; 1/2,500th second; f/6.3; ISO 1,250.

This day at Roath Park Lake was a photographer's dream. I managed to capture a thrilling coot battle up close, with one claw positioned right in front of the rival coot, intensifying the action. After persistent waiting, I was fortunate to be in the perfect spot at the right moment.

Catshark

Habitat | Highly Commended

Henley Spiers

Small-spotted catshark (*Scyliorhinus canicula*)
Shetland, Scotland

Nikon D850 with Nikon 28-70mm f/3.5-4.5 lens. 28mm; 1/15th second; f/16; ISO 800.

A spotted catshark swims over horse mussel beds in Shetland, one of the richest marine ecosystems in British waters. Also known as dogfish, they are the most most common shark in our waters but have long experienced a difficult relationship with humans. An early 20th-century text describes them as the 'foe of fisherman' who 'wages incessant war with their nets and catches'. Beachgoers are most likely to be aware of this shark through their egg pouches, which wash up on shore and are commonly known as 'mermaid's purses'. Despite their modest size, I find catsharks to be amongst the most beautiful of their species, with large eyes and intricate skin patterning. Note: Baiting with small amounts of mackerel chum used.

Beneath the Barrel
Coast & Marine

Lou Luddington
Barrel jellyfish (*Rhizostoma pulmo*)
Trefin, Pembrokeshire, Wales

Sony A7R II with Sony FE 28mm f/2 lens and Fisheye converter. 16mm; 1/320th second; f/11; ISO 640.

After a tip-off from friends, we headed to a spot on the north Pembrokeshire coast in the hope of seeing barrel jellyfish. It was Midsummer's Day; the water was clear, and the sun shone brightly. Pulling on our freediving gear and swimming out from the shore, we soon spotted them near and far – a gathering of 30 or more drifting and pulsating. Diving down, the view from below shows off the frills and cauliflower-like detail of their oral arms that bear many tiny mouths, each surrounded by stinging tentacles – the perfect setup for catching their miniature planktonic prey.

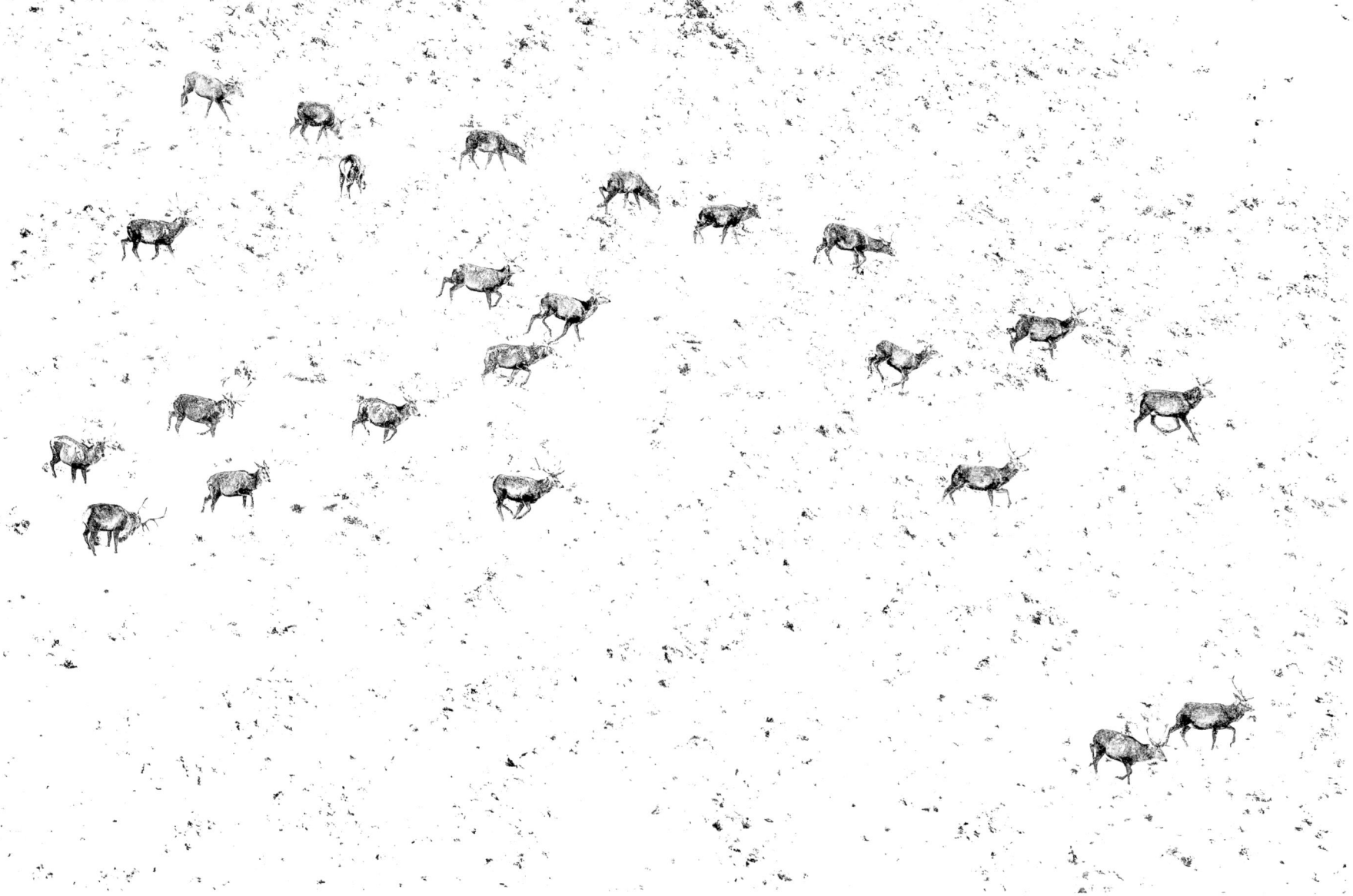

Primitive Winter
Black & White | Runner-up

Mario Suarez Porras
Red deer (*Cervus elaphus*)
Cairngorms, Scotland

Canon 5D Mark IV with Canon EF 100-400mm f/4.5-5.6L II lens. 400mm; 1/400th second; f/8; ISO 640.

I photographed this group of deer in the Scottish Cairngorms in the middle of winter. I overexposed four stops to create a contrast between the deer and the snow that could show an image with an artistic point of view, which strangely reminds me of the vision of the Great Hall of Polychromes of Altamira, a Spanish primitive cave whose paintings were the first European cave paintings for which a prehistoric origin was suggested and promoted.

Chasing Hares
Habitat

Paul Richards
Brown hare (*Lepus europaeus*)
Near Cley, Norfolk, England

OM System OM-1 with OM 300mm f/4 lens. 300mm; 1/2,000th second; f/4; ISO 400.

I like the photographic opportunity that 'bad' weather brings, often enhancing the atmosphere in a picture. In this instance, I was exploiting the snow and wind brought in by the storm and spent the whole day out in a Norfolk blizzard. I took advantage of the hares as they chased each other across the field with the wind whipping up the snow behind them. To approach, I used the cover provided by a hedge downwind of the hares and then crawled through to get the shot while lying in the snow-blown field.

Red Squirrel at Dawn
Habitat

Alastair Marsh
Red squirrel (*Sciurus vulgaris*)
Cumbria, England

Canon 5D Mark IV with Canon EF 16-35mm f/2.8L II lens. 16mm; 1/100th second; f/5; ISO 100.

I spend as much time as possible over autumn and winter with a local population of red squirrels in Cumbria. With huge thanks to a good friend of mine who puts hazelnuts out for them in his garden, I was able to take this remote wide-angle image of this squirrel at sunrise as the sun was burning through the clouds. They use this drystone wall to travel around the village, and I used one off-camera flash to illuminate the squirrel on its travels.

Through the Window
Animal Portraits

Tom Broxup
Little owl (*Athene noctua*)
York, England

Canon R5 with Canon EF 600mm f/4L II lens. 600mm; 1/800th second; f/6.3; ISO 1,000.

A friend once found an adult little owl drowned in a water butt and a small, unwell-looking owlet on the floor of an old sheep shed. When we investigated, the owlet was in poor condition. Luckily, the landowner's daughter was studying wildlife rehabilitation and we managed to clean its closed eyes. Unfortunately, it seemed the owlet had fallen from a roof cavity and there was no safe way to return it to the nest. We observed from a distance and saw that the remaining adult was struggling to find enough food for the owlets. To help, we put out mealworms. After an hour, the adult was flying in and out of the shed, feeding the owlets, especially the sick one on the floor. For three weeks, we scattered dead mealworms around the shed, and it was a joy to eventually see both owlets beginning to fledge. I started taking photos of them as they waited in the window for food. Setting up behind a hedge with my Canon R5 and 600mm lens, I captured the female and young in a relaxed pose in the shed window. It felt like a perfect ending to a rewarding project. This was one of the last images I took, as we stopped feeding them once they began hunting on their own.

Running Through the Heather
Animal Behaviour

Karen Miller
Mountain hare (*Lepus timidus*)
Monadhliath Mountains, Scotland

Nikon D850 with Nikon 500mm f/5.6 lens. 500mm; 1/800th second; f/6.3; ISO 400.

This image of a mountain hare running through heather was taken whilst I was on a hill with a couple of friends, my first visit since the first pandemic lockdown. I wasn't sure how many hares we'd find, as it's a tricky time of year and I'd been away for a while, but I was pleasantly surprised to spot a few. As we sat watching another hare, I noticed this one running towards us, not having spotted us sitting quietly in the heather. I was able to quickly amend my camera settings from static hare to running hare, upping the shutter speed to capture the action as it bounded across the heather directly in front of us.

Mountain Hare
Animal Portraits | Highly Commended

Chas Moonie
Mountain hare (*Lepus timidus*)
Findhorn Valley, Scotland

Canon 5D Mark IV with Canon EF 100-400mm f/4.5-5.6L II lens and 1.4x teleconverter. 560mm; 1/1,600th second; f/9; ISO 800.

I was lucky to pick a week in my native Scotland when deep snow in almost Arctic conditions was present. A steep climb up the track led me to several mountain hares which proved to be very confiding. This particular hare was running towards me, as it had spotted an eagle on the horizon, allowing me to capture a snapshot as it passed by.

◀ **Woodland Beauty**
Animal Portraits

Sheena Ramsay
Red deer (*Cervus elaphus*)
Highlands, Scotland

Canon R5 with Canon EF 500mm f/4L II lens. 500mm; 1/500th second; f/5.6; ISO 1,250.

On a wet winter's day in the Scottish Highlands, this beautiful red deer hind emerged from the forest and paused for a short time, briefly making eye contact before going on her way.

Snow Buck
Urban Wildlife

Alex Witt
Roe deer (*Capreolus capreolus*)
Surrey, England

Canon R6 with Canon EF 500mm f/4L II lens. 500mm; 1/1,000th second; f/4; ISO 250.

The snowfall arrived in late winter, which carried the added bonus of the roe buck sporting his large, newly grown, velvet-covered antlers, with the velvet to be shed in only a matter of a few weeks. After visiting the deer in the cemetery for several years and having grown quite attached to them while watching their progress throughout the seasons, it was great to finally come away with some images of the animals in a snowy winter wonderland, which had eluded me up until this point.

◀ **Sunlit**
Animal Portraits

Drew Buckley
Atlantic puffin
(*Fratercula arctica*)
Skomer Island,
Pembrokeshire, Wales

Canon R5 with Canon RF 100-500mm f/4.5-7.1L lens. 500mm; 1/1,250th second; f/7.1; ISO 800.

During an enjoyable evening on Skomer Island, as the sun started to set the light softened and warmed, allowing for lots of creative photography ideas. Positioning myself between the bird and the sun, I waited for the moment when it would flap its wings and capture the warm evening light shining through the outstretched wings. Even when shooting a burst of images, it's never a simple task to capture the moment, as puffins make all sorts of wonky wing shapes during their flaps; this one, however, came out relatively symmetrical.

Golden Eye
Animal Portraits

Lauren McIntyre
Roe deer (*Capreolus capreolus*)
Winchester, England

Nikon D850 with Sigma 150-600mm f/5-6.3 Contemporary lens. 600mm; 1/2,000th second; f/6.3; ISO 500.

I was sat on a field edge when suddenly a male roe came up the hill and casually entered the rapeseed field. He hadn't seen me, so I knew this was the moment to get my shot. I slowly crept along the edge of the crop to where he entered, trying to spot him before he spotted me. I noticed the antlers moving just above the crop, so I gently stood and lifted my camera to frame the shot. As he saw me, his head rose, and I took my shot before he leapt off into the sea of yellow.

Golden Compass
Animal Portraits

Lewis Jefferies
Compass jellyfish (*Chrysaora hysoscella*)
Falmouth, Cornwall, England

Sony A7 III with Sony FE 16-35mm f/4 lens. 16mm; 1/400th second; f/22; ISO 200.

I captured this image of a compass jellyfish floating at the surface under the low, golden sunlight on a flat, calm evening, with hardly a breath of wind and clear skies – a perfect midsummer's night. The warm light from golden hour matched the colour of the compass jellyfish and a burst of flash illuminated the subject, appearing as if the sun were lighting it and making the creature stand out against the inky dark water.

A Dance of Adders
Animal Behaviour

James Pearson
Adder (*Vipera berus*)
Sussex, England

Canon 7D Mark II with Canon EF 100mm f/2.8 Macro lens. 100mm; 1/1,250th second; f/5.6; ISO 800.

Before this photo was taken, I'd only seen adders dancing once for a fleeting moment. However, on this day I managed to find three separate pairs battling it out within the space of half an hour, which already made it a day to remember. It all came together when one particularly evenly matched pair was engaged in a duel for over 15 minutes, finally providing me with several unique photographic possibilities. Since they were more than preoccupied with each other, they completely ignored my presence, allowing me to get some photos I will cherish forever.

Three Wise Bats
Animal Portraits

Daniel Hargreaves
Lesser horseshoe bat (*Rhinolophus hipposideros*)
Cellar of a house in Dorset, a bat roost managed by the Vincent Wildlife Trust, England

Canon R with Canon EF 100mm f/2.8L Macro lens. 100mm; 1/200th second; f/11; ISO 400.

These winged wonders have individual personalities, as seen with the poses of this trio of lesser horseshoe bats. Adults weigh less than a 2p coin. In summer, females give birth to a single pup, and they can live up to 21 years. Equipped with incredible superpowers, they hunt flying insects and navigate in the dark. We can help them by switching off lights and reducing noise in their environment. Photo taken under licence.

Unison
Animal Behaviour

Csaba Tokolyi
Atlantic puffin (*Fratercula arctica*)
Skomer Island, Pembrokeshire, Wales

Nikon D800 with Nikon 70-200mm f/4 lens.
160mm; 1/400th second; f/4; ISO 640.

On the lush green cliffs of Skomer Island, three puffins engage in a lively dispute. Their vibrant orange beaks snap and squawk as they argue, each puffin standing its ground, eyes locked in a tense standoff. The rugged island, a sanctuary for a large puffin colony, provides the perfect backdrop for this animated avian quarrel amidst the thriving seabird community.

Daisy Daisy
Hidden Britain

Rory Lewis
Blue-tailed damselfly
(*Ischnura elegans*)
Cotswold Water Park,
Gloucestershire, England

Canon R7 with Laowa 90mm f/2.8 lens. 90mm; 1/200th second; ISO 320.

Damselflies are probably the insects that got me invested in macro photography to begin with; they are the epitome of how different an insect can look when viewed up close, and I have now spent many years capturing their hidden little personalities from different angles. The Cotswold lakes in South Cerney are a mecca for Odonata and in the early hours of the morning, you can be surrounded by hundreds of sleepy ones who pay no mind to your presence. This one was clinging to the stem of a large daisy, which I thought would make for an interesting scene, so I stretched out a large orange cloth on the ground behind it and used some clamps to bend the daisy closer to the ground. As I was getting into position, the damselfly started to wake, crawling to the top of the stem and onto the flower then waving its legs around in a sleepy attempt, it seemed, to continue climbing beyond. It stopped for a second, maybe when it spotted me, frozen briefly with one leg outstretched as if waving a friendly 'good morning'. I managed to fire off a good 45 exposures before it changed position, and although its leg was moving a little throughout the frames, I managed to retain enough detail when processing the stack to capture it pretty much as I saw it.

Banded Demoiselles at Sunrise
Hidden Britain

Jay Birmingham
Banded demoiselle (*Calopteryx splendens*)
Tamworth, Staffordshire, England

Canon R5 with Sigma 180mm f/2.8 lens.
180mm; 1/8,000th second; f/2.8; ISO 50.

I have taken a number of shots of banded demoiselles at sunrise, but this is the first time I have managed to capture two banded demoiselles with the sun rising behind. I was there quite a long time before sunrise and had worked out where the sun was going to rise. I then searched to see if there would be any in the right position and found these on some grass. I used a 180mm macro lens at f/2.8 to create a large disc of the sun around the demoiselles.

◀ **Bokeh Explosion**
Hidden Britain

Matt Smith

Chalkhill blue (*Lysandra coridon*)
Wildlife Trust Reserve, Kent, England

Fujifilm GFX 100S with Fujifilm GF 120mm f/4 Macro lens. 120mm; 1/320th second; f/11; ISO 400.

Having arrived early at the location, I found this chalkhill blue roosting and spent time observing its pre-flight preparations. The previous day had been hot, however, during the night, the temperature and wind dropped significantly, creating plenty of dew-drenched vegetation. By adopting a low angle and shooting into the rising sun and specular highlights on the vegetation, I created the bokeh/background effect. Being fairly early in the chalkhill blue season, I was really pleased to find one and have some beautiful conditions to photograph in.

Cave Crèche
Hidden Britain | Highly Commended

George Turner

European cave spider (*Meta menardi*)
Bissoe Valley Nature Reserve, Cornwall, England

Canon 90D with Canon EF 8-15mm f/4L Fisheye lens. 12mm; 1/100th second; f/4; ISO 2,500.

On a sunny day in August, while searching for subjects to photograph, I spotted some towering fireweed. Hoping to find some interesting insects pollinating them, I pushed through the dense foliage, uncovering a hidden mine shaft. Upon entering, I spotted some huge, perfectly preserved spider egg sacs hanging down from the beams and rocks above. To my disappointment, there were no spiders to be seen, so I continued inward. Distracted by the graffiti engraved on the wooden supports, I initially failed to notice an egg sac being protected by a cave spider until I looked up and saw it directly above my face! Ecstatic, I pulled out my fisheye lens and torch and began shooting. This was exciting, as I never expected to see a cave spider in a man-made mine shaft!

Dark Side
Black & White

Richard Beech
Moon jellyfish (*Aurelia aurita*)
Poole, Dorset, England

Sony A7R IVa with Sony FE 70-200mm f/2.8 GM II lens and 2x teleconverter. 336mm; 1/400th second; f/8; ISO 5,000.

The summer sun attracted jellyfish of all sizes to the lake's surface, so I decided to take a shot of the bloom from above as it created fascinating patterns. I used an aperture of f/8 to ensure some sharp details and chose one of the larger jellyfish to focus on. The mid-morning sun created some interesting light patterns on the water and the jellyfish seemed to be glowing, so I converted the shot to black and white, as I felt it better illustrated the intricate shapes of the jellyfish.

Ephemera
Black & White

Lou Luddington
Barrel jellyfish (*Rhizostoma Pulmo*)
Trefin, Pembrokeshire, Wales

Sony A7R II with Sony FE 28mm f/2 and Fisheye converter. 16mm; 1/320th second; f/7.1; ISO 500.

Glowing lampshade-like in the bright sun, these gently pulsating barrel jellyfish hunted mid-water for tiny plankton to eat. On Midsummer's Day, we set out in the hope of seeing them after a tip-off from friends. Snorkelling out from the shore, we soon spotted them near and far – a gathering of 30 or more fleshy alien beings drifting through space. Ephemeral in their passing, this was a remarkable encounter that will stay with me for years to come.

Leap of Faith
Animal Behaviour

Rich Bunce
Atlantic salmon (*Salmo salar*)
Yorkshire Dales, England

Canon R6 with Canon EF 24-70mm f/2.8L II lens. 50mm; 1/2,000th second; f/8; ISO 1,000.

I suspect many people would associate leaping salmon with Scottish waterfalls, yet with some local intel, good timing and a spot of luck, you can enjoy this spectacle in the heart of the Yorkshire Dales. Conservation work on the River Ribble has helped make this a more reliable spot to witness salmon and trout taking extraordinary leaps of faith. For this shot, I set up the camera on a tripod and fired with a remote every time I saw a hint of movement emerging from the white water.

Hunter, Hunted
Habitat | Runner-up

Sandra Stalker
Sea bass (*Dicentrarchus labrax*)
Balaclava Bay, Portland, England

Sony A7R IVa with Sony FE 28-60mm f/4-5.6 lens. 28mm; 1/100th second; f/20; ISO 1,000.

A sea bass hunts and patrols in amongst the thong weed and kelp. This image was taken in an area that although by the shore, due to it being next to a port can only be reached by boat, as a result whilst snorkelling it I observed large shoals of bass, existing undisturbed. There were shoals of juveniles so it is obviously an important nursery and then larger solitary bass hunting as this one was. To get the shot I had to hang in the water for about half an hour until the bass got used to my presence and then move really slowly. The visibility wasn't great so getting the shots without going to close was tricky as focussing through the milky water was hard. After three hours of snorkelling I managed one shot of a head on bass hunting.

◀ **Aerial Mugging**
Animal Behaviour

James Yaxley
Barn owl and Kestrel (*Tyto alba* and *Falco tinnunculus*)
St Benet's Abbey, Ludham, Norfolk, England

Canon R5 with Canon EF 500mm f/4L II lens and 1.4x teleconverter. 700mm; 1/2,000th second; f/5.6; ISO 1,250.

I'd seen this barn owl dive into the grass and catch a field vole. As it ate its catch, it constantly lifted its head between bites and surveyed its surroundings. Having previously seen kestrels stealing a barn owl's prey, I wondered if the owl's furtive behaviour was because a kestrel was nearby. With this in mind, I focused on the owl and waited in anticipation. Then, out of nowhere, a kestrel appeared and attacked the owl, sending feathers flying. However, despite the kestrel's attempted mugging, the owl escaped with its prey firmly clamped in its beak, minus a few feathers.

Angel Wings ▶
Animal Portraits

Rosalie Smith
Barn owl (*Tyto alba*)
Kent, England

Canon R5 with Canon EF 500mm f/4L II lens and 1.4x teleconverter. 700mm; 1/5,000th second; f/5.6; ISO 1,000.

As a lovely spring evening unfolded, I was hopeful for a glimpse of the barn owl, especially since they had young to feed, which increased my chances. Then, the magical moment arrived. I watched in awe as the barn owl hunted, suddenly turning and flying directly towards me. Coming eye to eye with these magnificent birds is always an unforgettable experience.

BRITISH SEASONS
DEER THROUGHOUT THE YEAR

I always get excited when I see a deer in the wild; it doesn't matter how common they may be or how often I see them – every time is like the first time.

They're magnificent, but also clever and quick. As they often spook easily and can hear or smell you from afar, I often find myself playing statues with them: when they're not looking, I move; when they are, I freeze. They make me work for my photos, but it makes it that much more rewarding when I get the shot.

Capturing the deer throughout the year was a challenge; planning to showcase the deer in iconic seasonal scenes is easy, but finding deer in those scenes was the tricky part. This is a collection that spans over four years and has taken a lot of patience, many near misses and a little helping of luck to achieve.

Spring
British Seasons | Winner

Lauren McIntyre
Roe deer (*Capreolus capreolus*)
Micheldever Woods, Hampshire

Nikon D850 with Sigma 150-600mm f/5-6.3 lens. 600mm; 1/500th second; f/6.3; ISO 1,000.

In spring, things come alive: the flowers start to bloom, the deer lose their winter coats and everything in general becomes more colourful. One of the most iconic flowers in spring is the wild English bluebell, so I knew a roe deer in bluebells would make an iconic seasonal photo. I came across this deer as it was sitting amongst some poorly lit bluebells. I waited, hoping he would move, and after about 40 minutes he rose and slowly moved into a nicer spot and even looked up for a brief moment, resulting in the beautiful spring scene I'd imagined.

Summer
British Seasons | Winner

Lauren McIntyre
Roe deer (*Capreolus capreolus*)
Hampshire, England

Nikon D850 with Sigma 150-600mm f/5-6.3 lens. 600mm; 1/1,600th second; f/6.3; ISO 1,250.

Summer brings taller crops, which make the deer harder to find and photograph. Poppies are an iconic summer flower, so I knew it would make a good summer photo; however, finding a poppy field is tricky, and finding a deer in one would be twice as tricky. As I arrived at the field, a roe was just settling down for a nap in the middle of it. After a couple of hours, his head appeared above the poppies. Thankfully, despite the crop being tall, the deer was taller, so I could get my summer photo of the roe amongst the poppies.

Autumn
British Seasons | Winner

Lauren McIntyre
Red deer (*Cervus elaphus*)
Bushy Park, London, England

Nikon D750 with Sigma 150-600mm f/5-6.3 lens. 600mm; 1/640th second; f/6.3; ISO 800.

Autumn sees the temperatures change and the foliage turns to those iconic yellow, orange and red colours. It's also the season of the deer rut for the red deer – a time for bellowing, duelling, and courting. There was no doubt about my autumn photo; I knew exactly what I wanted, I just needed the right conditions and a willing participant. As the sun rose behind this proud stag, it highlighted his breath – another bonus to the early morning autumn temperatures. The stag stood looking out across the area, protecting his females, with a lovely orange autumnal glow surrounding him.

Winter
British Seasons | Winner

Lauren McIntyre
Fallow deer (*Dama dama*)
Winchester, Hampshire, England

Nikon D850 with Sigma 150-600mm f/5-6.3 lens. 460mm; 1/2,000th second; f/6; ISO 640.

Snow is, of course, the iconic weather for winter. The personal problem I had is that I live in Hampshire, where it hardly ever snows, so this photo required some patience and luck. There has been a single day of proper snow in the last three years here, so when snow appeared in the forecast, I knew I couldn't waste it. With a stroke of luck, I stumbled across a herd of nine fallow deer playing in the snow, one white stag amongst them. I photographed him running, and it just felt like I was watching reindeer play. Finally, I had my winter photo.

DOCUMENTARY SERIES
LAND USE – HUMAN ACTIVITIES AND ITS IMPACT ON MARGINALISING THE NATURAL WORLD

In 2023, the UK was declared one of the most nature-depleted countries on Earth. Viewing my Land Use portfolio begins to provide insight into why this is the state of nature in our country.

Around 2019, I started to experiment with camera-drone nature photography and its storytelling potential quickly became apparent. While the bird's-eye view of the natural world was difficult to interpret initially, I quickly understood the aesthetic and realised its documentary potential in recording how human activities impact natural environments. My Land Use project portfolios often draw criticism for not including 'nature', but that's sort of the point, isn't it?

Arable Deserts
Documentary Series | Winner

Chris O'Reilly
Derbyshire, England

DJI Mavic 2 Pro. 28mm; 1/60th second; f/4; ISO 100.

The industrialisation of the landscape is embodied here – monoculture symmetry, hard-cropped hedgerows and hemmed-in field margins, all functioning to maximise crop yields. Farming this intensely decimates biodiversity, releases carbon stores and depletes soil nutrients, thus threatening future food production. I strove to juxtapose a landscape photography aesthetic against the brutally stark reality of nature depletion.

Nature Corridors
Documentary Series | Winner

Chris O'Reilly
Derbyshire, England

DJI Mavic Air II. 28mm; 1/100th second; f/5.6; ISO 100.

A disused canal dissecting a housing estate and farmland provides a very important nature 'corridor' which supports flora and fauna and, of course, human wellbeing too. Converted into a footpath and left in a semi-managed state, the canal transects the landscape for miles, benefiting many species by joining up fragmented wilder habitats.

Island Copse
Documentary Series | Winner

Chris O'Reilly
Inverness-shire, Scotland

DJI Mavic 2 Pro. 28mm; 1/80th second; f/3.5; ISO 100.

The strong symbolism in this image serves as a metaphor to illustrate mankind's dominance over nature. The tractor tracks encircling the beleaguered remnant of woodland isolate the copse as a hostage within a man-made environment. The strong composition choice further enhances the impact of the story.

Light-catchers
Documentary Series | Winner

Chris O'Reilly
South Yorkshire, England

DJI Mavic 2 Pro. 28mm; 1/4th second; f/8; ISO 100.

Heralded as the UK's answer to bolstering energy security, renewable energy has become central to the strategy. Solar capture undoubtedly has a part to play in reducing global CO^2 emissions, but is further 'urbanisation' of our natural estate the correct approach, especially with so much urban real estate available?

Wind-catchers
Documentary Series | Winner

Chris O'Reilly
Aberdeenshire, Scotland

DJI Mavic 2 Pro. 28mm; 1/4th second; f/8: ISO 100.

Aesthetically pleasing or a blight on the landscape, whatever your view, wind farms are here to stay. Noise disturbance, habitat loss and bird strike collisions are often cited in protests against wind farm installations. Overlooked tends to be the impact on natural environments of the support infrastructure required.

Progress?
Documentary Series | Winner

Chris O'Reilly
Derbyshire, England

DJI Mavic 2 Pro. 28mm; 1/160th second; f/5.6; ISO 100.

Brown hares, redpoll, linnet, nesting skylark and lapwing, in addition to rich communities of insect and plant life, all used to frequent this area. The industrial complex that now occupies the landscape is regarded to have delivered 'progress' to this former 'greenfield' site. The industrialisation of landscapes is a major contributor to the UK's nature deficit issue.

YOUNG BRITISH WILDLIFE PHOTOGRAPHER OF THE YEAR

Curlew O'clock!
Young British Wildlife Photographer of the Year 2025 and 11 and under | Winner

Jamie Smart
Eurasian curlew (*Numenius arquata*)
Wiltshire, England

Nikon Z 9 with Nikon Z 800mm f/6.3 lens. 800mm; 1/1,250th second; f/6.3; ISO 720.

It was a very early morning start and a four-hour drive to try to get the early morning light on the plains. As the sun was just coming up over the hill, I noticed how it caught the dandelion clocks and lit them up like little fuzzy lamps everywhere. I was lining up my camera out of the car window, ready to capture a photo, when I heard a curlew nearby. I scanned the area to try to find where they were and found this one wading through the dandelions just in front of me.

I See Trees of Green…
11 and Under | Runner-up

Tyler Hood
Sparrowhawk (*Accipiter nisus*)
Norwich, England

Canon 70D with Sigma 150-600mm f/5-6.3 lens. 600mm; 1/80th second; f/6.3; ISO 100.

For a couple of years, one of my goals was to get a more 'natural' shot of a sparrowhawk, one in a natural habitat and looking relaxed. And I got lucky. During a walk inside a small local park, I heard the call of a male alerting the female that he had food. I stood at a distance and observed for a little while and was able to learn that this branch he landed on was, in fact, the branch they were using to food pass to each other. The male would land and call loudly until the female came and took the food. I decided to get a little closer, hid behind a big bush and got in position so that the leaves were around the hawk, giving a perfectly green and natural look. It's exactly what I had dreamed of! I took a few shots and then left so that they would not get disturbed! What a lucky day.

Call of the Wild

11 and Under | Highly Commended

Flynn Thaitanunde-Lobb

Red fox (*Vulpes vulpes*)
Southampton, England

Nikon D850 with Nikon 70-300mm f/4.5-5.6 lens. 300mm; 1/500th second; f/5.6; ISO 320.

I spotted this female fox one evening and realised the field was home to her and her family. She sat on the grass in the same spot most evenings, waiting for the rest of her family to return. She had raised a young fox earlier in the year, and recently I saw another little cub, who did not seem to mind me. The adult male, however, kept a watchful eye on me, as if assessing whether I was a risk to his cub. Thankfully, he concluded that I posed no risk and he lowered himself onto the grass and relaxed.

Street Cleaners
15-17 years | Winner

Ben Lucas
Feral pigeon (*Columba livia domestica*)
Essex, England

GoPro HERO 8. 3mm; 1/350th second; f/2.8; ISO 100.

When I found a packet of fries someone had abandoned, I knew that it wouldn't be long until it attracted opportunistic pigeons. I set up a small GoPro camera in the back of the packet, and after some very weird looks from people passing by, the birds finally started to show up. As they approached the food, I triggered the camera with voice commands so I didn't put the birds off their meal and I pulled off this shot. Our carelessness removes the natural food for many species and provides for others. These birds are truly the vultures of the streets.

Kissing Hares
15-17 years | Runner-up

Joe Dagger

Brown hare (*Lepus europaeus*)
Warminster, England

Canon 7D Mark II with Sigma 150-600mm f/5-6.3 Contemporary lens. 150mm; 1/4,000th second; f/7.1; ISO 1,250.

I've always noticed two hares frequenting the field bordering my grandparents' garden. Despite numerous attempts, capturing them on camera had been elusive. However, on this particular occasion I was determined to succeed. Hastily returning to the house to grab my waterproof gear and camera, I patiently crawled towards the hares. After reaching a safe distance, I waited patiently, allowing them to acclimate to my presence. Eventually, they grew comfortable enough to approach me, moving gracefully together. It was then that I zoomed out on my lens, capturing an intimate moment between them against the backdrop of their natural habitat.

Lazing About
15-17 years | Highly Commended

Anton Poon

Grey squirrel (*Sciurus carolinensis*)
Buckinghamshire, England

Canon R7 with Canon RF 100-500mm f/4.5-7.1L lens. 500mm; 1/400th second; f/7.1; ISO 5,000.

I decided to take a walk with my camera around my school grounds and noticed a squirrel among the tall grass foraging and exploring the area. Slowly, the squirrel made its way towards a tree. I followed, careful not to disturb the squirrel, finding the animal splayed out on top of a branch. It was a hot day, and the sun was shining through the foliage behind. The squirrel was seemingly exhausted from the heat and its foraging, now taking a break in the tree. I moved to capture the moment, taking care not to interrupt the squirrel's rest.

And Take-off – Gannets at Bass Rock
12-14 years | Winner

Kiran Simpson
Northern gannet
(*Morus bassanus*)
Bass Rock, Scotland

Sony a1 with Sony FE 200-600mm f/5.6-6.3 G lens. 600mm; 1/3,200th second; f/7.1; ISO 800.

It was an incredible experience to spend my 13th birthday surrounded by the thousands upon thousands of gannets that populate Bass Rock. I was fortunate enough to capture a particularly special moment: a shard of light pierced through the cliffs just as a gannet was flying off to fish. It was a magical scene that made the day unforgettable – a birthday I'll cherish forever.

Red Kite Fishing

12-14 years | Runner-up

Jack Brackley
Red kite (*Milvus milvus*)
Horn Mill Osprey Hide, Oakham, Rutland, England

Sony A7R III with Sigma 150-600mm f/5-6.3 Sports lens. 262mm; 1/2,000th second; f/6.3; ISO 2,000.

I visited a site in Rutland in the hope of seeing ospreys fishing, but instead I enjoyed the unexpected sight of a red kite doing something of an osprey impression! I was amazed to watch this one pick up a fish in its talons and fly towards me, and I had to react quickly with my 200-600mm lens and use a fast shutter speed to capture the action.

Curious Deer

12-14 years | Highly Commended

Eilidh Shannon
Roe deer (*Capreolus capreolus*)
Aberdeen, Scotland

Canon 70D with Sigma 150-600mm f/5-6.3 Contemporary lens. 562mm; 1/800th second; f/6.3; ISO 1,250.

The day that this photo was taken, I was at Aberdeen golf course, which is surrounded by the sea on one side and high-rise flats on the other, right in the middle of the city. I had a tip-off that there were short-eared owls there, stopping to refuel on their journey. While I was searching for them, this roe deer appeared through the long grass. It is amazing to see how much wildlife you can find even in the city, showing that you don't have to travel far to find the wonders of nature.

INDEX

Kirsty Andrews 18, 161
instagram.com/kirstyjandrews

Billy Arthur 84
lonabrakphotography.co.uk

Will Atkins 55

Andrew Bailey 118

James Ball 105
instagram.com/james.wildlifeworld

Wendy Ball 129
flickr.com/photos/wendy_ball/

Rosie Barrett 79
rosiebwild.co.uk

Richard Beech 216
richardbeechphotography.com

Jay Birmingham 213
jaybirmingham.com

Dan Bolt 165

Jack Brackley 239

Peter Brooks 158
peterbrooksphotography.co.uk

Paul Browning 26
paulbrowning.photography

Tom Broxup 76, 201

Drew Buckley 17, 37, 42, 58, 117, 206
drewbuckleyphotography.com

Rich Bunce 65, 218
walkingphotographer.co.uk

Simon Carder 167
simoncarderphotography.com

Matthew Cattell 92
matthewcattellphotography.com

Vai Meng Chan 62
instagram.com/jokerchan

Bret Charman 93
bretcharmanphotography.com

Paul Colley 35
riverphotographer.wordpress.com

Robert Collins 32
instagram.com/robert_lewis_c0llins

Amanda Cook 15
instagram.com/amandacook5321

Mark Cooper 148
instagram.com/markccphoto

Tim Crabb 39
buggedbeyondbelief.com

Joe Dagger 237
instagram.com/jdaggerphotos

Sarah Darnell 69, 113
sarahdarnell.photography

Eden Davies 29

Finley Dennison 27, 61
instagram.com/finleydennisonphoto

Robin Dodd 70
fastfoxphotography.com

Max Ellis 98
maxphotographic.com

Charles Everitt 192
charleseveritt.com

Marc Freebrey 97
instagram.com/marcfreebrey

Andrew Fusek Peters 139
fusekphotos.com

Jonathan Gaunt 123
instagram.com/jonathangauntphoto

Tim George 163

David Gibbon 90

Matthew Glover 48

Paul Goldstein 94, 119, 176
paulgoldstein.co.uk

Gina Goodman 140
instagram.com/ginagoodman

Danny Green 68
dannygreenphotography.com

Ben Griffin 71
instagram.com/griffagram

Jacob Guy 141
jacobguymedia.com

Phill Gwilliam 31
instagram.com/phillipgwilliam

Ben Hall 14, 172
benhallphotography.com

Daniel Hargreaves 210

Christopher Harrison 41
charrison.photography

Chris Hawes 56, 103, 127, 150, 154, 171

Deborah Hockey 110, 131

Tyler Hood 234
instagram.com/tylerhoodphotographs

Jane Hope 114

Amy Humphries 67
instagram.com/amyhumphries_shots

Tim Hunt 54
timhuntphotography.co.uk

Helen Jackson-garside 188
helenjgphotography.co.uk

Phil James 178
instagram.com/philjames_naturephotography

Lewis Jefferies 208
lewismjefferies.myportfolio.com

Tom Kelly 122, 153
gowildinedinburgh.co.uk

Harry King 194

Mark Kirkland 21
instagram.com/markunderwater

Jed Lawson 152
instagram.com/j.lawgraphy

Rory Lewis 212
instagram.com/invertebrain

Robin Lowry 51, 53
instagram.com/robin_o_lowry

Ben Lucas 236

Lou Luddington 197, 217
louluddington.com

James Lynott 24, 183
jameslynott.smugmug.com

John Macfarlane 135
instagram.com/johntmacfarlane

James Mackinnon 7
instagram.com/mackinnon_capture

David Maitland 9, 23, 49, 75
davidmaitland.com

Philip Male 174

Lee Mansfield 73

Gillian Marsh 19

Alastair Marsh 102, 107, 128, 200
alastairmarsh.co.uk

Ben Marsh 187
instagram.com/benmarshphoto

Stuart Martinez 66

Ian Mason 104, 130, 168

Brian Matthews 184

Jamie McDermaid 173
jamiemcdermaidphotography.co.uk

Roy McDonald 99, 169

Neil McIntyre 47, 77, 185
neilmcintyre.com

Lauren McIntyre 30, 40, 134, 207, 222–225
instagram.com/laurenmcintyre.photography

Karen Miller 202
www.karenmillerphotography.co.uk

Justin Minns 182
justinminns.co.uk

Chas Moonie 46, 203
wildfeathers.uk

Nicholas More 25

Robin Morrison 81
flickr.com/photos/68911555@N03

Andrew Neal 166
andrewneal.gallery

Takaki Nemoto 88
natureneedsnologo.com

Mark Nicolaides 43
aboutdeer.com

Graham Niven 38, 162
nivenphotography.com

Chris O'Reilly 226 - 231

Lee O'Dwyer 116

Francesca Page 146
francescapageart.com

Steve Palmer 109
stevepalmer.photography

Andy Parkinson 80
andrewparkinson.com

James Pearson 209
instagram.com/jpearsonphotography

Heshan Peiris 155
instagram.com/heshpeiris

Richard Peters 125

Paul Pettitt 44

Rachel Piper 52, 136
rachelpiper.me.uk

Anton Poon 237

Ben Porter 115
benporterwildlife.co.uk

David Pressland 180
davepressland.myportfolio.com

Sheena Ramsay 204

Paul Richards 199
pronature.co.uk

Gordon Roach 87
gordonroachphotography.co.uk

Jeremy Robbins 57, 63
jeremyrobbins.co.uk

Thomas Roberts 36
instagram.com/spottedthroughlens

James Roddie 16, 89, 100, 138, 164, 190
jamesroddie.com

Andrew Rouse 186

Christopher Rutter 191
chrisrutterphotography.com

Andy Sands 91
andysands.co.uk

Paul Saunders 85

Kevin Sawford 86
kevinsawford.com

Diana Schmies 151, 179

Philip Selby 59, 83

Eilidh Shannon 239

David Shawe 96
davidshawephotography.com

Richard Sheldrake 108
richardsheldrakephotography.co.uk

Kiran Simpson 238
instagram.com/kiran.simpson

Jamie Smart 232

Rosalie Smith 132, 142, 221
rksimages.co.uk

Matt Smith 214
oakspringphotography.com

David Southern 60
southernphotography.co.uk

Henley Spiers 20, 196
henleyspiers.com

Sandra Stalker 143, 219
instagram.com/teenytinyunderwaterphotos

Martin Stevens 147
wildlifevision.com

Jenny Stock 34, 137
jennystockphotography.co.uk

Stephen Street 193
stephenstreet.co.uk

Matt Stuttard Parker 170
mattstuttard.co.uk

Mario Suarez Porras 198
instagram.com/mariosuarezporras

Saleel Tambe 120
saleeltambe.com

Julian Terreros-Martin 10
instagram.com/julian_terrerosmartin

Flynn Thaitanunde-Lobb 235

Mike Tibbotts 124, 149
instagram.com/miketibbotts

David Tipling 156, 157
davidtipling.com

Csaba Tokolyi 211
csabatokolyi.com

Daniel Trim 111, 112
instagram.com/danieltrimphotography

Nur Tucker 45
nurtucker.com

George Turner 74, 215
instagram.com/gerder.nature

Syed Muhammad Irtiza Usman 195
instagram.com/irtiza_bokhari

Michael Van Wegen 121
michaelvanwegen.com

Martin Vaughan 126

Alison Vaughan 181

Ian Wade 95, 145, 177
ianwadewildlife.com.com

John Waters 160
johnwaters.tv

Matthew Watkinson 50
mostlypuffins.com

Michael Watson 82
mickwatsonphotography.com

Norman Watson 101
normanwatson.co.uk

Jacob J. Watson-Howland 133
jacobwatsonhowland.com

Dave Wesson 28

Terry Whittaker 22, 189
www.terrywhittaker.com

Sarah Williams 144
sarahwilliams.zenfolio.com

Liam Willis 72
instagram.com/mrliamwillis

Simon Withyman 12, 64
keepitwild.co.uk

Alex Witt 33, 78, 205
alexwittphotography.wordpress.com

Andrew Wood 159
woodforthetr33s.com

Ian Wood 175
agoodplace.co.uk

James Yaxley 106, 220
www.jamesyaxleyphotography.co.uk